Beginners Guide To Woodworking

An Introduction To Basic Hand Tools, Equipment, And Techniques In Starting Your Woodworking Journey

Kirk Andersen

© **Copyright Batpatch Enterprise 2022 - All rights reserved.**

The content contained within this book may not be reproduced, duplicated or transmitted without direct written permission from the author or the publisher.

Under no circumstances will any blame or legal responsibility be held against the publisher, or author, for any damages, reparation, or monetary loss due to the information contained within this book. Either directly or indirectly. You are responsible for your own choices, actions, and results.

Legal Notice:

This book is copyright protected. This book is only for personal use. You cannot amend, distribute, sell, use, quote or paraphrase any part, or the content within this book, without the consent of the author or publisher.

Disclaimer Notice:

Please note the information contained within this document is for educational and entertainment purposes only. All effort has been executed to present accurate, up to date, and reliable, complete information. No warranties of any kind are declared or implied. Readers acknowledge that the author is not engaging in the rendering of professional advice. The content within this book has been derived from various sources

By reading this document, the reader agrees that under no circumstances is the author responsible for any losses, direct or indirect, which are incurred as a result of the use of the information contained within this document, including, but not limited to, — errors, omissions, or inaccuracies.

Table of Contents

Preface	1
Introduction	3
Chapter 1 - Understanding Wood	7
Chapter 2 - Shop Safety	21
Chapter 3 - Hand Tools	27
Chapter 4 - Power Tools	41
Chapter 5 - Joinery	45
Chapter 6 - Finishing The Project	55
Chapter 7 - Woodworking Plans	67
Bird Feeder	71
Bird House	83
Squirrel Feeder	89
Paper Towel Holder	95
Napkin Holder	101
Taco Shell Holder	107

Preface

When I started my own journey into woodworking, there was no Internet (at least not as we know it today), and I was having difficulty finding resources that were truly for the beginner. Apart from a hand saw and hammer, I had no idea what tools were needed in starting my woodworking journey.

It's been roughly 15 years since I started that journey, and most of my knowledge has been self-taught by trial and error (more error than trial). I understand how encountering problems can be hurdles that prevent those from starting or continuing on a woodworking journey. That is the purpose of this book, to encourage those who are on the starting line of this joyful journey of woodworking to continue the pursuit.

I call woodworking a journey because it never stops, you are constantly learning new things no matter your experience level. I also found woodworking to be my personal therapy of the grind of everyday life, and it's my desire to encourage others to embark on this journey.

Beginners Guide To Woodworking

Introduction

First, let's ask the question, "What is woodworking?" Of course, the basic answer is to be working with wood. But that is not the whole answer. There are many different professions and hobbies that work with wood that are not considered "woodworkers." One profession that always comes up is a carpenter, and many people get carpenters and woodworkers confused. Yes, they both work with wood, but a carpenter works on a job site building a structure of some sort, such as a house or other type of building, while woodworkers work mainly in a shop and create useful items to put in the house. Steve Ramsey, of "Woodworking for Mere Mortals," has an excellent definition of woodworking:

"Woodworking is a productive craft that involves cutting, shaping, and joining wood to create decorative and/or useful things."

With an understanding of what woodworking is, the next question is who are the woodworkers of today? It wasn't that long ago that seeing a woman in a woodshop was an anomaly, but not anymore. The stereotypical woodworker of the past, such as the elderly grandfather tinkering in the garage building a birdhouse, is no longer the case. Woodworkers today come from every facet of society, from an executive of a large company to the person grinding it out stocking shelves. It is the desire to make things with their hands that they have in common.

Most woodworkers I know do it for two main reasons: they like making things with their hands and just enjoy it. If you thought that most woodworkers did it to save money by building things themselves, that is actually low on the list of why they do it. Also, it may surprise you if I told you that most things that woodworkers make they could probably buy cheaper than it costs them to make, although the quality and craftsmanship won't be the same. It isn't the cost savings that attracts people to woodworking, it's the joy of building something yourself and the pride in showcasing it and telling others that "I built that."

Now that we understand what woodworking is let's talk about the different types of woodworking. Although there are many different types of woodworking, they fall under two primary categories, hand tool woodworking, and power tool woodworking.

Most woodworkers today fall under the latter category of power tool woodworkers. There are many advantages to using power tools. First of all, the skill level required to use power tools is much lower than hand tools, and of course, it takes a fraction of the time to cut a piece of wood on a table saw than with a hand saw. This time savings does come at a cost. It's more dangerous to operate a power saw than a hand saw, so shop safety is of utmost importance (Chapter 2 covers shop safety). Cost is not that much of an issue as today's power tools are very affordable, and you can start building projects right away. Most woodworkers actually use a blended style of woodworking, in which they use hand tools for certain applications and power tools for others.

With all that being said, this book is dedicated more to the use of hand tools. Don't get me wrong, if I have a choice of using a hand tool or a

Introduction

power tool, I will reach for the power tool the majority of the time, but I also believe that using hand tools in developing a person's understanding of woodworking techniques is far better than using power tools. In future volumes, I'll go more in-depth into the use of power tools.

Since this book is geared to the true beginner in woodworking, there are some topics that will not be covered here but will be covered in future volumes as the woodworker progresses in their journey. This includes how to set up a shop, as most people just starting out may not have a dedicated space to do woodworking. I started my journey in the corner of a one-car garage, but you don't even need that much room when starting out. Just find a suitable location to conduct the work and have all your tools in a box, and pull them out as you need them. Just be mindful that many operations, such as sawing (especially with a power saw) and sanding, tends to create a lot of dust that goes everywhere, so I highly recommend not to perform these operations inside your house. If you don't have a garage (or other suitable location), it is best that these operations be conducted outside.

Beginners Guide To Woodworking

Chapter 1
Understanding Wood

In order to understand how the lumber in your shop will behave once you start working with it, it is essential to know how wood is produced, from how a tree grows, to being harvested and then milled into lumber.

It would be fair to say it is common knowledge that wood comes from trees. But it would also be fair to say that the average person has little knowledge of how wood behaves. The way a tree grows has a direct impact on the lumber that's produced from a tree. Many factors influence how a tree grows, from the wind, the amount of sunlight it receives, the amount of shade, soil condition, the amount of rainfall, and competition with neighboring trees all have an impact. Not only will lumber from different trees behave differently, but lumber from different parts of the same tree will behave differently. With an understanding of how wood behaves, a skilled craftsman can quickly determine if a particular piece of lumber will be a good fit for their project.

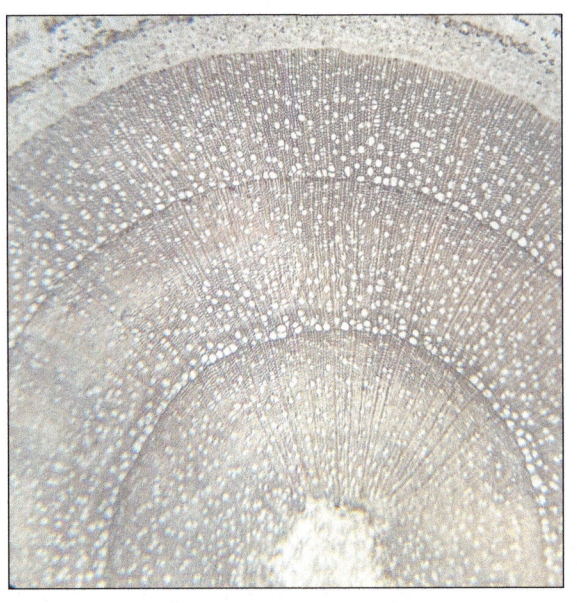

As with all living things, wood is made up of cells that are clustered together. The cells in wood are long and bundled together, which is what creates the grain we see in wood. This can be demonstrated by taking a bunch of straws and gluing them together. Individually each straw is weak and easy to bend, but once they are bundled together, it becomes very difficult to bend the straws. It is, however, relatively easy to pry them apart. This is the same principle as to why wood splits easily along the grain, but is rigid across the grain.

When looking at a cross-section of a log, you can see the different layers of growth. On the very outside is the bark, this is the tree's protective layer. The bark is usually removed during milling as it has very little value to woodworkers. The next layer is the sapwood, this is where most of the tree's nutrients are transported. Next is the heartwood, this is the oldest part of the tree, in some species like cherry and walnut, the heartwood usually has a deep vibrant color compared to the

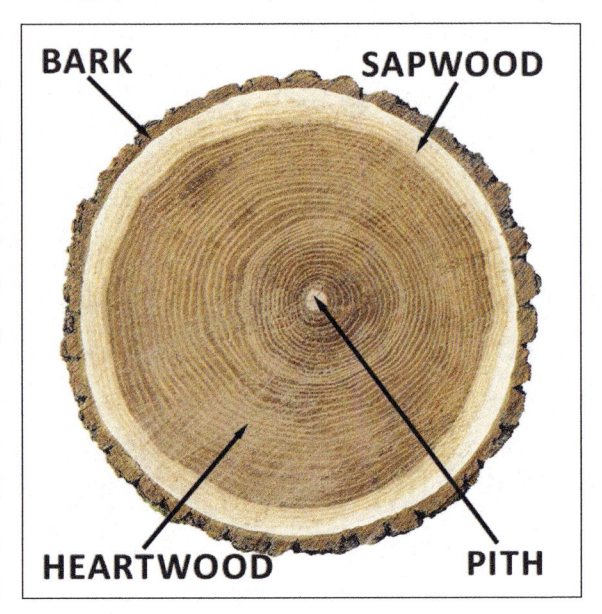

Chapter 1 - Understanding Wood

sapwood. The heartwood also has a lower moisture content and is harder than the sapwood. At the very center of the tree is the pith. Lumber with the pith in it is the least desirable, as it is extremely unstable.

Regardless of what the wood will be used for, we want it to be relatively dry. When a tree is freshly harvested more than half its weight is water. Before any wood can be used, the majority of the moisture needs to be removed. A good piece of lumber to work with should have a moisture level between 8-10%. Most of the issues that we encounter with wood is due to its moisture level. Since wood is very porous, it will swell in a high moisture environment and shrink in a low moisture environment. But this swelling and shrinking only occurs to the cell's diameter, it does not affect the cells length. Therefore, wood only changes in size across the grain and not with the grain. If left to nature, a log will slowly dry from the outside inward, resulting in the outer portions of the log shrinking long before any interior cells would dry. This results in the log developing cracks or splits in its external areas. The same effect would result if milled lumber were left to dry naturally. This can be avoided by drying the lumber in a controlled environment.

An area that needs to be addressed is the end grain of lumber. Since the cells on the end of a board have been cut open, they are more susceptible to the effects of moisture. They will absorb and release moisture at a faster rate than the intact long grain cells. This results in the ends of the boards cracking and splitting. To avoid this, the ends need to be sealed prior to being dried. This is done by either painting or waxing the ends. Now you know why the ends of lumber you buy may be painted.

Once the lumber has been milled, it is now ready to dry. There are two ways lumber is dried, either naturally (called air-dried) or in a kiln (called kiln-dried). No matter which method is used, the lumber needs air to circulate all around each board in order to control the drying process. The boards are first stacked with spacers or sticks in between them, this process is called "sticking." When air-drying lumber, it needs to be placed in a location that does not receive direct sunlight, this would result in the areas of the boards that are in the direct sunlight drying faster than the rest of the board, resulting in, you guessed it - splitting. One of the most significant issues with air-drying is the time it takes. On average, it takes one year to dry each inch of a board's thickness, so if you had some 4" X 4"s you wanted to use, you would need to wait four years to use them.

Roughly 75% of the lumber sold has been kiln-dried. Just like air-drying, the lumber first needs to be stickered, it is then placed in a large kiln where both heat and humidity are regulated. The humidity is slowly reduced as the temperature is slowly increased. Going to fast could result in, yep, splitting. Depending on the wood species, it can take 1-2 months to kiln dry 1" thick lumber down to 8% moisture content, which is a slow process, but it is still faster than the one year it would take to air dry. However, a good portion of kiln-dried lumber is dried to only 15-18%, which takes only a few days in the kiln.

Now let's talk about different types of wood. Although there are many wood species, they can all be placed into one of two broad categories, softwoods and hardwoods. As a rule, softwoods come from trees that produce cones and have needles that stay green all year, while hardwood trees shed their leaves each year. Since I live in the United States, I will be talking about woods that are native to the United States, just use whatever woods that are native to your area. Popular softwoods in the United

Chapter 1 - Understanding Wood

States are pine, fir, spruce, and redwood, and some common hardwoods are oak, cherry, walnut, maple, and ash. Although the rule of thumb is that softwoods are softer than hardwoods, that is not always the case. An example is basswood, which is classified as a hardwood, but is softer than pine.

Most furniture is made from hardwoods, this however is not a rule that must be strictly adhered to. But there is no doubt that a table made of oak will handle wear and tear better than one made from pine. On the other hand, softwoods, such as pine, are more likely to be seen at a construction site rather than hardwoods.

Now let's talk about how logs are milled into lumber. There are many different types of milling operations, ranging from mills that produce millions of board feet a year, to small sole proprietor mills operating portable lumber mills. Now you're asking, what is a board foot? A board foot is a unit of measurement used in determining the size of a board of wood. One board foot is a board that is 12" wide by 1' long and 1" thick. The mathematical formula in determining this is to multiply the width (in inches) by the length (in feet), then divide that by 12 (12" in a foot), this gives you the square foot of the board. Then you need to multiply that number by the thickness (in inches) and that will give you the board foot. An example is a board that is 8" wide and 6' long and 1.5" thick has a total of 6 board feet. This example would look like this: 8 x 6 = 48; 48 / 12 = 4; 4 x 1.5 = 6.

I do hope that didn't confuse you as much as it did me at first. The reason you need to understand how to calculate a board foot is for when you buy lumber. The majority of the time, lumber is sold by the board foot, unless you're making your purchase at a big box store. I won't say I never buy wood at a big box store, but the majority of the wood I purchase is either from small mills or specialized lumber retailers.

Now back to the actual milling. A log can be milled in many different ways, and the way they're milled determines the final lumber product. I could write a whole book on how a sawyer cuts a log, but as a woodworker we're more concerned with the end product. The first type of board that we will talk about is the most common you will encounter; it is called flatsawn boards. Flatsawn boards are the easiest and most efficient method of cutting a log. These boards are easy to identify with their arching end grain pattern and flaming pattern on the boards face. The main issue with flatsawn boards is that the grain pattern of each face is different, this creates opposition between each face, resulting in a board that is somewhat unstable and susceptible to warping (we will go further into the different types of warping a little later).

Chapter 1 - Understanding Wood

The next board type is the quartersawn board. These boards are the cream of the crop and are identified by a vertical end grain pattern and straight parallel lines on the face grain. These boards are the most stable since each board's face is identical, creating no opposition between the faces. Many woodworkers like using quartersawn boards not only for their stability but also for the board's aesthetics. Milling quartersawn boards results in waste that could have produced more flatsawn boards and is more labor-intensive for the sawyer, resulting in a higher cost for the woodworker.

Riftsawn boards are similar to quartersawn boards. The face of a riftsawn board looks very similar to that of a quartersawn board. The difference is identified in the end grain, while the end grain of a quartersawn board is vertical, a riftsawn board's end grain will be at an angle. Riftsawn boards are more stable than flatsawn boards but not as stable as quartersawn since the faces are not identical.

The last type of board we will talk about are boards with pith in them. As already mentioned, the pith is the center of the tree and is extremely unstable. You usually only see a board with the pith in it in large diameter boards such as 4" x 4" or 6" x 6". The reason is that the mass surrounding the pith in these boards helps stabilize the board, making them usable for certain applications, such as fence posts. You will however find 2"x4"s in the big box stores with the pith, just avoid these boards.

13

As I previously mentioned, there are many small mills in operation, and many of them have portable mills and will come to your location and mill your trees on site. Although they usually won't cut down the tree, as the tree will already need to be down. As far as the question of drying the lumber, they may also offer this service, or you may need to figure that out on your own.

Most of the logs milled are for veneers. A veneer is a very thin sheet of wood that ranges from 1/8 inch to 1/100 inch in thickness. There are two ways veneers are milled; rotary cutting and flat slicing. A rotary cut veneer is produced when the cutting blade cuts the veneer as the log is spinning. Theoretically, this would produce one very long veneer. Flat sliced veneers on the other hand are cut while the log is stationary as the cutting blade slices the veneer. Rotary cut veneers are primarily used in plywood manufacturing, while flat sliced veneers are usually stacked into what is called a flitch. Since a flitch is stacked in the order it was cut from the log, the grain patterns and coloring of the veneers match, therefore flitches are widely used by furniture makers.

Now that we've talked about how natural lumber is milled, it's time to switch to engineered lumber (also referred to as man-made lumber). There are many types of engineered lumber, we're only going to concentrate on two of them: plywood and particleboard.

Plywood is manufactured by stacking veneer sheets. The sheets are rotated from each other so that the grain of each veneer sheet is 90 degrees from one another. This rotation of the grain is what gives

Chapter 1 - Understanding Wood

plywood its strength and stability. No matter the thickness of plywood, each sheet is made up of an odd number of veneers (or plies), this ensures that the grain pattern runs in the same direction on both exterior faces. Standard thicknesses of plywood range between 1/8 inch to 3/4 inch, although there are specialty plywoods that are outside this range. Not all plywoods are created equal. How plywood is manufactured depends on what the particular plywood will be used for. Other than the type of wood used, the biggest difference between plywoods is the number and thickness of the plies used in its manufacturing. For example, most construction-grade 3/4" plywood is made from pine and may only have five plies, while a cabinet-grade 3/4" baltic birch plywood may have as many as 15 plies. Another difference is any voids that may be present. A void is an area within the plywood where there is no wood, this results in a weak area within the plywood. It is common to have voids in construction grade plywood, while higher grade plywood is relatively void free.

When it comes to particleboard there are many varieties, but they are all made from the same basic components; wood chips and glue. What differentiates each of them is the size of the wood chips and the pressure used to compact them in the manufacturing process. The most common types of particleboards are oriented strand board (OSB), medium-density fiberboard (MDF), and hardboard.

OSB is very easy to identify by the large wood chips used in its manufacturing. Although OSB is used in some woodworking applications, such as making cabinet carcasses, it is predominantly used in the construction industry.

On the other hand, both MDF and hardboard are made with an almost powdered wood chip. This also means that more glue is needed in the manufacturing process, resulting in a much denser and heavier product. MDF is very stable, will stay true and straight, holds screws well, and takes paint nicely. But when it comes to handling the sheets, especially when it comes to 3/4" sheets, MDF is heavy and hard to work with without having someone assisting you. But once you're able to maneuver the sheets, it is easy to cut, but it is also very dirty. What I mean by dirty is it creates a lot of very fine dust when it is cut, and this dust goes everywhere. A good dust mask is a requirement whenever cutting MDF. There are a few downsides to MDF and hardboard, first the edges are fragile and prone to chipping, and when they get wet, they will swell like a dry sponge dropped in a sink of water.

Now that we have an understanding of how lumber is produced let's talk about what the wood can do once it gets to your shop. I can guarantee you that every board you bring into your shop will warp to some degree, some of the warping won't be noticeable at all, while others will make you wonder if it's the same board you brought into the shop.

Wood boards can experience five basic types of warping, some of them you can mitigate and work around, while others there's nothing to do but shrug your shoulders and go find another board. Before going further in-depth, the basic warps are bowing, crooking, cupping, twisting, and kinking.

Chapter 1 - Understanding Wood

Bowing is when the board deviates from being flat lengthwise but not across the board's width.

Crooking is where the edges are no longer in alignment.

Cupping is when the face of the board deviates across the board's width.

Twisting occurs when all four corners are no longer on the same plane.

And lastly, kinking is when a board's edge deviates somewhere along the board.

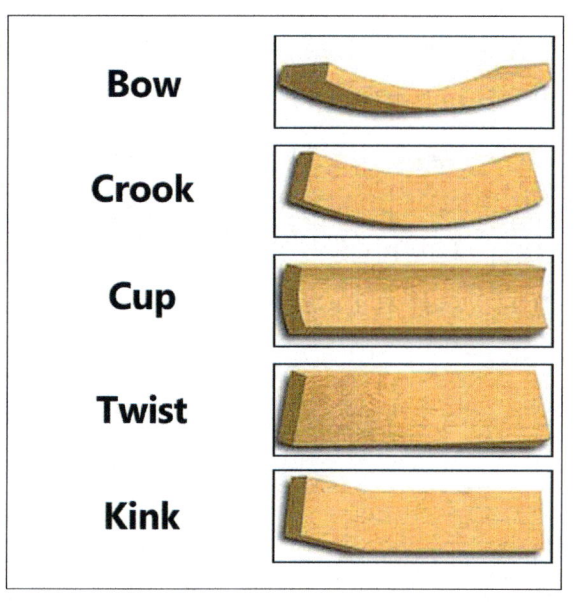

As discussed earlier, warping occurs when wood experiences a change in its moisture content. Knowing this, there are a few precautionary measures that can be taken to minimize warping, but there is no way to totally eliminate warping. The first thing you can do in minimizing warping is in your choice of wood for your project, as some woods have reasonably straight grains which are less susceptible to warping, these include redwood, fir, and cedar. If you noticed, these are all softwoods, so if your project requires a hardwood, this may not apply. If your project will be made from a hardwood, try and get quartersawn wood, as it is more stable and less prone to warping. Of course, this may be an issue if you are in an area that doesn't have any hardwood retailers. Just do what you can with what you have available.

No matter where you purchase your wood, whether it be at a lumber yard, big-box store, or a specialty wood dealer, I can guarantee you that when you bring the wood to your shop, it will be in a different environment and has the potential of acting totally different than when it was at the store. There is no way that the humidity and temperature of your shop are identical to that of the store.

You should always try to plan your build at least a day or two in advance and never purchase wood the same day you plan on working with it, you need to give the wood time to acclimate to its new environment. This acclimation period should be at least two days, but a full week would be better. I can't tell you the number of times I've put a straight piece of lumber in the shop to come back a day or two later to find it looking like a pretzel. The difference in humidity is always the culprit.

We can't control what the wood will do, but we can control the extent of how this will affect the wood within reason. This is done by ensuring the wood doesn't acclimate to its new environment unevenly, as uneven acclimation is the main issue that leads to warping. There are ways to minimize any uneven shrinking or swelling the wood will experience. When new wood is introduced into your shop, the first thing that should be done is to "stick" it, just like the sawmills do. This will ensure that there is even airflow around the wood while it is acclimating to the shop's environment. If you were to place a board directly on a surface without spacers, the area of the board that's in direct contact with the surface will not acclimate to the environment at the same rate as the area of the board that is open to the environment. Another thing that is helpful is to have a fan lightly blowing on the boards to keep the air constantly circulating around them. There is nothing you can do that will 100% prevent any warping, but this greatly reduces the effects of warping.

Although you can't see it, wood is constantly under tension and this tension only reveals itself after the board has been cut. This tension is usually counter balanced within the board itself, but this counterforce is removed or interrupted once the board is cut. Although we don't go into operating a table saw in this book, whenever cutting a board on the table saw that has tension in it, it can be extremely hazardous, as this is one of

Chapter 1 - Understanding Wood

the main issues that produces kick-back on a table saw (we will get more into table saw operations in a later volume). But since you can't see the tension until the board is being cut there is no way to prepare for it, that is why you should always cut every board as if it is under tension. There are a few things that can happen when cutting a board that's under tension. Either the cut ends can come together like tweezers and pinch the saw blade, or they can spread apart. Another thing that can occur is that the board can curl. I was cutting a board a while back on the table saw that was straight as an arrow, when I finished the cut, it looked like a rocker from a rocking chair.

It is also important to understand how wood is graded. Since most softwoods are primarily used in the construction industry, they are graded on the wood's structural strength. Hardwoods on the other hand, are graded at the sawmill. The criteria used in grading hardwoods are based on the width of the board, the proportion of sapwood on the better face, and the yield after cutting out knots. At the top of the grading scale are Firsts and Seconds (FAS), then Select and Better, followed by #1 Common and #2 Common. But be aware that just because wood is graded at FAS doesn't mean every board will be at the standards you want, it is always nice to be able to sort through lumber to find the pieces that fit your project.

Now, don't get grading confused with rough-sawn or surfaced boards, just because the board may have been surfaced doesn't mean it is a higher grade. It just means the wood has been planed in order to remove saw marks and has a smooth finish. Rough-sawn lumber will still have the saw marks from it being milled. If you have the tools to surface boards yourself, buying rough-sawn boards can be a better option because they will be thicker and cheaper. The last thing I want to talk about lumber is its thickness. Lumber is classified in thickness by quarters, meaning if you want a 1" board, it would be labeled as 4/4 (four quarters), and a 1.5" board would be 6/4 (six quarters), and so on.

There are many types of woods available, although there will always be recommendations for what woods to use or not use in a particular project, it ultimately comes down to your preference as the craftsman.

Chapter 2
Shop Safety

Shop safety is a topic that always seems to be overlooked or is just an afterthought by many. I believe that safety is of the utmost importance. With that said, I also don't believe in and totally dislike the slogan "Safety First." This ideology of mine probably comes from the years I served in the Navy. The majority of my time in the Navy was onboard submarines, and if safety always came first, we never would have left pier side, never mind submerging the boat. I prefer the adage "Think Safety," as safety always needs to be at the forefront, but the task at hand is the primary concern. When it comes to safety, we need to determine what is the desired outcome and how we can achieve that in the safest manner possible. A quick example, I was cutting a very small piece of wood on the table saw, but after evaluating the situation, I determined it couldn't be cut safely on the table saw, so I decided to cut it with a hand saw. Are there risks in using a hand saw? Of course, but the risks are much lower than using the table saw. The task was completed, which was the primary concern, and in the safest manner possible.

When it comes to working in the shop, the first thing we need to do is prepare ourselves mentally to be in the shop. What this comes down to is making sure we are well-rested and alert. It also goes without saying that we don't want to be under the influence of any substance, be it alcohol or drugs. If you are taking any medication that warns about operating any machinery, please think twice about being in the shop.

Next, we need to prepare ourselves physically to be in the shop. Since most power tools spin in one fashion or another, this creates a cutting hazard or has the potential of grabbing an item and pulling it into the spinning device. You don't want to be wearing any baggy clothes that could get pulled into these tools. But it's not just power tools that you need to be cogent of, I can't think of a single hand tool that doesn't have the potential of inflicting injury.

There are some clothing that is recommended to be worn in a shop, and others that should be avoided. Long pants, closed-top shoes (safety shoes would be ideal), and a short-sleeved shirt are all recommended, although some may argue long sleeved-shirts would be better in providing protection for the arms. The issue, in my opinion, is that long sleeves have the potential of getting caught in the machinery. If you do wear long sleeves, just roll up the sleeves. Jewelry of any kind should not be worn in the shop. There are instances where someone has lost a finger, or worse, because they didn't take off their jewelry.

Eye Protection

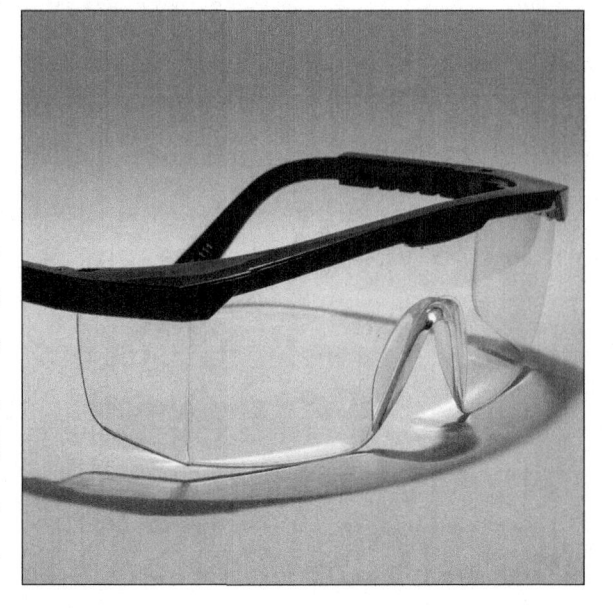

When we're in the shop, there's some personal protective equipment (PPE) items that need to be worn before we can start certain operations. One item that should be worn during most operations, whether using the table saw or a hand saw, is eye protection. There are three basic types of eye protection: Safety glasses, safety goggles, and a full-face shield. If you're going to use safety glasses, it is recommended that you get ones that wrap around the face to give some protection from projectiles coming in from the sides. In my opinion, full-face shields don't provide the type of eye protection needed in a shop, they are just too open around the sides. They are more designed for a lab environment to protect you from liquids splashing in your face than from fast-moving projectiles. My personal choice of eye protection is safety goggles. They provide maximum protection all-around your eyes. The downside with goggles is they tend to fog-up.

Dust Mask

Protecting our lungs is of the utmost importance during any operation that creates dust. Some woods create dust that on their own is toxic, but let's put that aside. Prolonged exposure to any wood dust can cause serious health concerns. A dust mask should be worn when operating any power tool that creates airborne dust, which is basically every power tool. Even when using some hand tools, a dust mask should be worn. You wouldn't believe the amount of air-borne dust created while just hand sanding.

Not really part of the PPE conversation, but it is relevant. Whenever you're using power tools that create dust, they should be connected to some sort of dust collection system. This can be as simple as hooking the tool up to a shop-vac or it can an elaborate piping system that goes to a central dust collector. Even making one cut on a 2X4 with a circular saw will fill a room with airborne dust. If you don't have any dust collecting capability, it is recommended that you do as much of this type of activity as possible outside.

Hearing Protection

The level of sound that some power tools create is ear-shattering, so we need to wear ear protection when operating these tools. There are two main types of hearing protection: Earplugs and earmuffs. Earplugs are made from either a soft foamy or rubbery material and are designed to go into the ear canal. They conform to the canal, thus blocking noise from entering the inner ear. Earmuffs (often called Mickey Mouse Ears) go around the outside of the ear. They are made up of two hard plastic shells that go over the ears and are connected by a head strap that goes over the head to hold the shells in place. The inside of the shells are lined with sound-absorbing foam, and the rims of the shells have foam padding for both comfort and to allow the shells to conform to the wearer's head. Earmuffs are also easier to remove and since they are bigger than earplugs, they are easier to find when you forget where you put them.

Gloves

You should also have a pair or two of good-quality work gloves available. Gloves protect your hands from splinters when handling wood, and I don't care how big a man (or woman) you are, you get a nice splinter in the palm of your hand, you will scream in pain (been there, done that). But what you don't want to do is wear gloves while operating any tools (specifically power tools), as you want to feel what the tool is doing, and if you're wearing gloves, you won't be able to.

Shop Apron

Another piece of PPE that is recommended but is not a requirement is a shop apron. Aprons do two things. First, they provide an additional layer of protection to your body, and second, they provide pockets for you to put things. We've all heard of, or better yet have experienced it ourselves, the dilemma of "where is that pencil I had just a minute ago." Most shop aprons are usually made from heavy materials, such as denim, canvas, or leather.

Shop Safety Equipment

Within the shop itself, there are a few items that are a necessity. Every shop needs to have a fire extinguisher in it. I don't think I need to go into detail as to why this is important. Another item that needs no explanation is a first aid kit.

Another item that is totally overlooked as being safety-related is a broom. Keeping the shop floor clean is important, as the build-up of sawdust on the floor can be quite slippery. To go along with the broom is a shop-vac. As already mentioned, a shop-vac can be used for dust collection on certain power tools. Rags and/or paper towels are always a good idea to have available in the shop as you never know what spills you may need to clean up. Don't forget disposable gloves, these are extremely useful when applying finish to your project. Not only will they protect your hands from the solvent in the finish, but they also keep your hands clean, so you don't need to scrub off three layers of skin to wash them.

In concluding with shop safety, I'm going to go back to my Navy days again, you can have all the safety equipment in the world, but if you don't use them, what good are they. And lastly, the number one piece of safety equipment in the shop is YOU.

Chapter 3
Hand Tools

It's finally time to talk about the tools we will be using in our woodworking journey. As I've already mentioned, this book is devoted to using hand tools, although we will talk briefly about some power tools in the next chapter. With the proper hand tools, you can do anything that can be done with power tools, although it will take longer. Another difference between hand tools and power tools is that hand tools tend to be more specialized in that they may be designed to do only one specific task, while power tools tend to be more versatile. A good example is if you want to cut a dado (we will cover what a dado is a little later), to cut it by hand, there are planes specially designed for that, and they do an excellent job, but for any other type of operation they are just paper weights. On the other hand, there are some power tools that are excellent options for cutting a dado, such as a table saw or router and they're also capable of performing many other operations.

Suppose you really want to get into woodworking with only hand tools. In that case, I say go for it, as many hand tool techniques are being lost, just be mindful that the skill level needed for many hand tool techniques can take years to master, but if you're like most of us (and that includes myself) doing woodworking purely with hand tools is not the journey we're on. Now with that, not only I do believe it is important to learn how to use hand tools but learning proper techniques with hand tools provides a better understanding of the technique and how wood behaves. It is then relatively easy to adopt these techniques to power tools.

I've broken down certain hand tools into two lists, the first list consists of hand tools that I deem as required to build the projects in this book. The second list are tools that would be nice to have but not a necessity. Now let's start with the required hand tools.

Hand Saws

The saw is by far the most used tool in any shop, whether it be a hand saw or power saw. There are countless books written on just hand saws and how to use them, this section won't even scratch the surface. There are three basic types of hand saws: Panel saws, back saws, and frame saws. There are many sub-categories within each type and each hand saw is designed to perform a specific tasks.

Traditional hand saws are designed as either ripping or crosscutting saws. Both crosscutting and ripping saws have their teeth bent slightly away from the center of the blade (in formal terms, the blade is referred to as a plate, not to offend anyone but I will continue to call it a blade), but a crosscutting saw has the edge of its teeth angled (sharpened) on the inside, resulting in the teeth slicing through the wood like a knife, while ripping saws don't have this feature. To understand the reasoning for this, let's go back to the example of using straws in demonstrating the composition of wood. In crosscutting, there are many layers of cells you're attempting to cut through, as opposed to ripping where you're cutting along the cells or with the grain. There are hybrid tooth configurations designed for both ripping and crosscutting, called "Sash" tooth, but these are not as proficient as a crosscutting or ripping configured saw. But it is an option if you can only afford one saw. With all that being said, a crosscutting saw can be used to rip, and a ripping saw can be used to crosscut, it just won't provide as clean a cut.

Another important thing to consider when selecting a hand saw is the number of saw teeth per inch (TPI), this can also be referred to as points per inch (PPI). Saws with larger teeth are usually for ripping, while saws with smaller teeth are for crosscutting. Saws with large teeth will quickly cut through wood, although saw marks will be left behind on the wood, and it can be difficult to get accurate, precise cuts. On the other hand, you can achieve an accurate, precise cut with saws that have smaller or fine teeth, and they will leave a relatively smooth cut, although it would not be a practical choice for long cuts.

Panel Saw

The panel saw is what most people think of when we say hand saw. This is the stereotypical saw with the enclosed grip handle, a thin metal blade that tapers, and saw teeth on one side. A saw like this can be the backbone of a woodshop, but it is limited in what it can do proficiently. This style of saw is called by many names from softback saw, long saw, panel saw, western-style saw, or just plain "hand saw." The blades on these saws are flexible, which is why they are sometimes called "softback" since they don't have the rigid back of a backsaw. The teeth on a ripping panel saw averages 4-7 PPI, while a crosscut saw averages 7-9 PPI.

Back Saw

Back saws are so-called because they have a rigid strip of brass or steel on the back edge of the thin blade, this keeps the blade rigid, which makes it the perfect saw for making precise accurate cuts. They also have very fine teeth resulting in smoother cuts. The tooth count ranges from 11 to 20 PPI. Back saws are specifically designed for joinery as they can produce very fine cuts. Back saws are the type of saws most often used with a miter box.

Miter Box

Not a saw, but used with a saw, a miter box is a device that allows you to make precise angled cuts. Miter boxes can be made of plastic, metal, or wood. Some of the simplest miter boxes only allow you to cut 90 or 45-degree angles, while more elaborate ones allow you to cut multiple angles. You can use most any saw with most miter boxes, but it is best to use a backsaw.

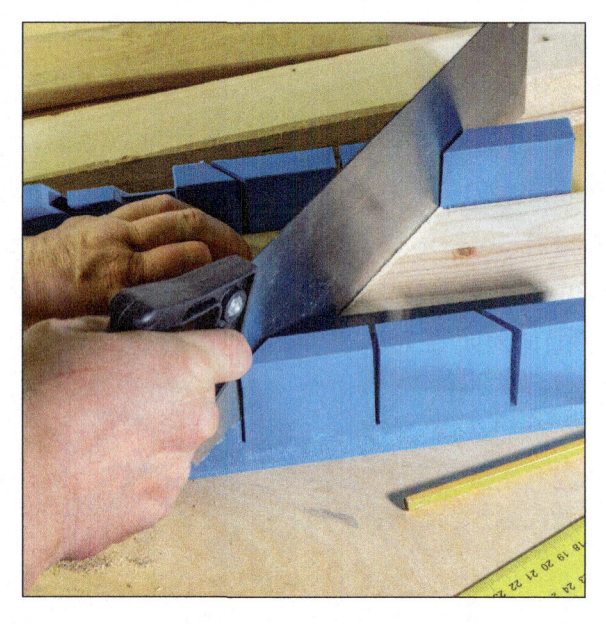

Frame Saw

There are many different kinds of frame saws, they usually have a narrow blade stretched from one side of the frame to the other. They can either be an open frame, with only three sides, and the blade is stretched across to make up the fourth side, or a closed frame. Closed framed saws tend to be very specialized, and unless you intend to pursue traditional hand tool woodworking, you may never use or even see a closed framed saw.

Chapter 3 - Hand Tools

With that, every framed saw is a specialized saw, and there are only a few that every woodworker should have. The first frame saw that is a must is a coping saw, this saw has a very narrow blade designed to make curved cuts. Another frame saw that is nice to have around is a hacksaw. Although hacksaws are primarily designed to cut metal, you can get wood cutting blades for it, and there are times when you may need to cut some metal.

Specialty Saws

There are a few specialty saws that don't fit in any of the above categories. A flush trimming saw and a veneer saw are two examples. The only one that I recommend as a nice-to-have saw is the flush trimming saw. The flush trimming saw has a very flexible blade with fine teeth, this allows you to trim pieces of wood sticking out without severely damaging the wood it is protruding from.

Push vs. Pull

The last topic about saws that needs to be discussed is the difference between push and pull saws. If you're from the western part of the world, you are most likely more familiar with a push saw, in that the cutting action occurs when you push the saw away from you, they are commonly referred to as western-style saws. While a pull saw's cutting action occurs when you pull the saw towards you, they are often referred to as Japanese-style saws. To resist binding up while being pushed through the wood, western-style saws have much thicker blades than pull saws. Since the Japanese style saws have thinner blades, they create a narrower cut, called the kerf. An advantage of the Japanese Ryobi saw is that it has teeth on both edges of the blade, one edge is for crosscutting and the other for ripping, so you only need one saw. Also, the handle on the Japanese-style saw is similar to a sword handle, allowing you to use both hands while cutting, which significantly reduces fatigue. With all the advantages of the Japanese style saw, if I were to have only one saw in the shop, it would be the Japanese style Ryobi. However, there are times when a western-style saw would be a better option since they usually have larger teeth. It would be a better choice when doing long ripping cuts. The best scenario would be to have both types in your arsenal.

Hammer

Possibly the oldest tool in recorded history is the hammer. It would be extremely difficult, if not impossible, to drive a nail into a piece of wood without a hammer. There isn't a workshop in the world that doesn't have a hammer (or two or three). Hammer handles come in many different materials and shapes. There are even hammer handles that have tuning forks in them to reduce the vibrations going to your hand. Those are designed for people who are using a hammer all day, every day. Just find one that is comfortable in your hand. As far as weight, I recommend a 16 oz hammer, it is kind of the standard, and most people can handle a hammer of this size without any issues.

Screwdrivers

A good screwdriver is a must in the shop. Although the majority of the screw driving done in shops today are done with the drill, there will always be times when the drill is not the best option, such as in tight areas where the drill won't fit or when dealing with small screws and a drill would overdrive and strip the screws. There are many options available, but with all the different types of screw heads, it is good to get a screwdriver with interchangeable screwdriver bits. That way, you don't need a separate screwdriver for a slotted, phillips head, square head, or star head. Again, find one that is comfortable in your hand.

Chisels

A chisel is a cutting instrument with a long metal blade of 4" – 6", with a flat back and beveled sides. A chisel is designed to cut wood either by chopping or slicing. Chopping is usually done by striking the end of the chisel handle with a mallet, while slicing is usually accomplished by the user pushing on the chisel. A chisel should be very sharp and should be sharpened periodically, even a new chisel should be sharpened prior to use. When cutting certain joints, such as a half-lap joint with a circular saw (or hand saw), it will leave a very rough surface. A chisel is needed to smooth out the surface of these joints. That is why I have chisels listed as a required tool.

Sharpening Stones

A sharpening stone is listed as a required tool since even a new chisel should be sharpened prior to being used, and you can't sharpen a chisel without a sharpening stone. There are many ways to sharpen chisels, you can use a grinder or specialty tools designed just for sharpening chisels. A sharpening stone is by far the most cost-effective. Another item that will be needed is a jig to keep the chisel at the correct angle while sharpening, as it is basically impossible to maintain the correct angle by hand.

Layout Tools

In order to make good cuts with your saw, you first need to mark where that cut needs to be made. There are a plethora of devices on the market to assist you in laying out your patterns. The majority of them are just nice to have tools to make it easier. In my opinion, there are only a few required tools to get the job done, they are: Tape measure or folding ruler, combination square, speed square, protractor, pencil, and blocks of wood. Some nice to have items are: Machinist's squares, calipers, dividers/compass, sliding bevel gauge, and countless others.

Tape Measure/Folding Ruler

To make accurate measurements, you need a tape measure or folding ruler. The most prevalent measuring device is the retractable steel tape measure, although there are some issues with them, they are by far the cheapest and easiest way to measure something, and they come in various lengths, from 3' to 25' (or more). The biggest issue with them is the hook on the end, if it's banged around a lot, this can affect its accuracy, there are also plenty of examples of the hook being attached incorrectly during manufacturing affecting their accuracy up to half an inch. Now, if you take all your measurements from the same tape measure all the time, then that's not a huge issue, but if you're like most woodworkers who have multiple tape measures floating around the shop, it most definitely can create problems. They are also limited in where they can go. Try making an accurate measurement on the inside of a box, it becomes frustrating at times. Most folding rulers are made of wood and unfold to 6'. I will have to admit that the folding ruler takes me back to my childhood as my father was a handyman, and all he used was a folding ruler (and he would get mad at me when I would use it as a toy). In certain situations, the folding ruler may be a better option. In my opinion, get both.

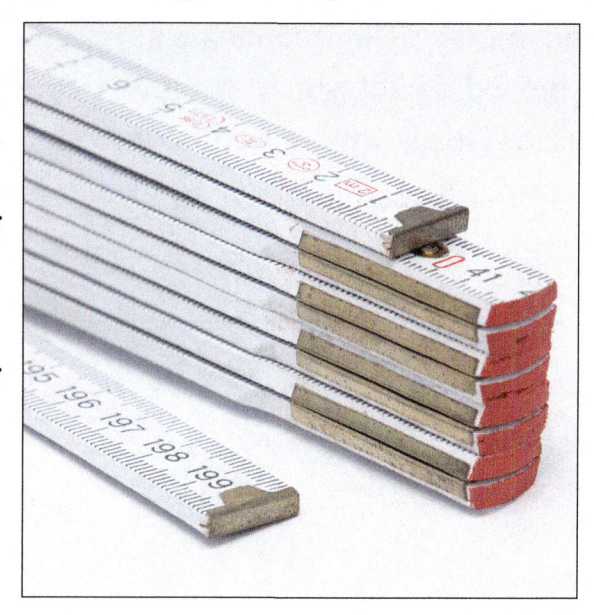

Combination Square

The combination square is a multipurpose measuring device. Not only are you able to mark out both 90 and 45-degree angles, but it can be used to find depth, draw layout lines, used to adjust the blade and fence on a table saw, and more. The ruler can also be removed, giving you a straight edge ruler. This is why it is considered a required tool; it is so versatile.

Speed Square

The speed square, or rafter square, was developed to assist roofers in building a roof. Although there are many uses of a speed square, there are two that make it a required tool for our purposes. First, it can be used as a guide to a hand saw or circular saw, ensuring you get a perfect 90 or 45-degree cut. The second is when you're gluing up your project to ensure that your joint is at a perfect 90 degrees, and with the opening in the middle of the square, you can get some clamps in there to ensure the joint stays at 90 degrees as the glue cures.

Chapter 3 - Hand Tools

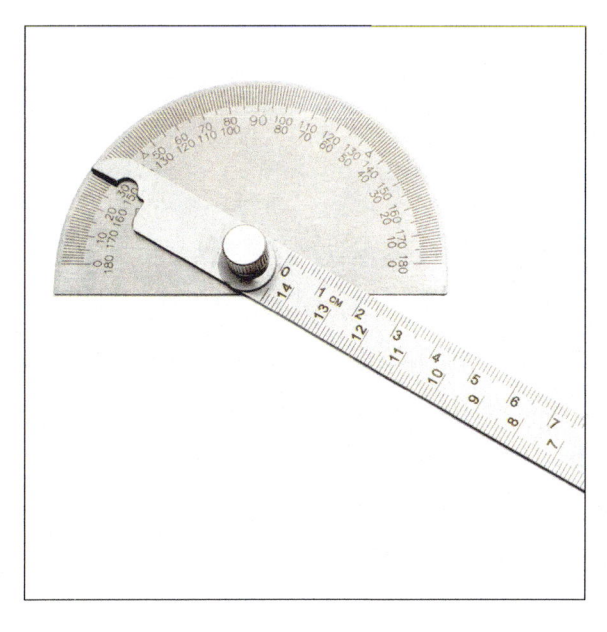

Protractor

A protractor is needed to draw layout lines of different angles. As discussed earlier, you can layout 90 and 45-degree angles with either the combination square or speed square, but there are times (many times) when you need to lay out different angles, and for that, you need a protractor. I'm not talking about the plastic half circle protractor from your school days, this protractor has a square (or rounded) head with an adjustable arm.

Pencil

All the measuring tools in the world are useless unless you can mark your measurements. Introducing the pencil. You can use any kind of pencil as long as it has a fine point, as you want your marks to be as precise as possible. You don't want a mark that is 1/4" wide. There are those that say a mechanical pencil is best. I personally prefer a regular wood pencil. You just need to keep the pencil sharp with a good pencil sharpener. What kind of pencil you use is a personal choice. What I do not recommend are the square carpenter pencils, as the lead (it's actually graphite) is just too wide.

Blocks of wood

When I say blocks of wood, what I'm referring to are spacer blocks. When you're building a project with pieces at identical intervals, instead of measuring out each piece's location individually, use a spacer block to set the pieces. Once you have one piece set, just use a spacer block to set the next piece, and so on. Theoretically, when using spacer blocks, you may not need to use a tape measure in assembling your project (the only time you would need a tape measure would be to measure the spacer block).

Can of Beans

Yes, I said can of beans. When you need to make curved layouts and don't have a compass, there is nothing better than a trip to your kitchen's pantry for a can of beans (or whatever your preferred vegetable is for that day).

That concludes the list of my recommended required tools. Now let's talk about some tools that didn't make the required list but would be nice to have.

Hand Planer

Hand planers are designed to take off a thin slice of wood. They're excellent at chamfering a board's edge, flattening a twisted board, and countless other operations. Although there are many specialty planes, there are two main categories: Bench planes and block planes. Bench planes are the longest of the planes, they can be over 2' long, but average between 9" to 22". Because of their size, they are ideal for smoothing large surfaces. Block planes are much smaller and can be designed for specific tasks, such as cutting dados (as previously mentioned). It takes some time to be proficient in using a hand plane, which is one reason they are only a nice-to-have item.

Machinist Square

Machinist squares are 90-degree metal squares that usually come in a set of four. The sizes in most sets are 2 3/8", 3", 4" and 6". These squares didn't make it to the required list since the combination square is already on it. They make it on to the nice to have list because of their size, as they can fit in tight areas that the combination square can't. And they're also nice looking.

Calipers

Calipers, no not the kind that goes on your car's wheels, are measuring devices used to measure an object's diameter. The read-out can be digital, dial, or rule scale. They are especially useful at measuring small objects. Again, a nice to have tool.

Compass

The compass is a drawing instrument used to draw circles and arches. This tool could be a required item (as they can be relatively inexpensive), but the can of beans won that slot for our purposes.

Sliding bevel gauge

The sliding bevel gauge is used for setting and transferring angles. The simplest ones have an adjustable arm that can be tightened down with a lock nut, or you can get a more elaborate one with a digital display of the arm's angle. Whatever kind you get, they can be quite useful, but they are still only a nice to have item.

This concludes the chapter on hand tools. There are many more tools that didn't make it onto either list, as the purpose here was not to tell you about all the tools that are available but to introduce you to the basic tools needed to start your woodworking journey. In future volumes, you will be introduced to more tools needed to continue on your journey.

This chapter was just to give you an introduction and brief description of certain hand tools, details on how to use the tools will be explained in the plans chapter of this book.

Chapter 4
Power Tools

Since this book is dedicated to the use of hand tools, this will be a relatively short chapter. There is, however, one power tool I do consider as a requirement: a power drill. There are also a couple of other power tools that are nice to have when building projects in this book; a circular saw, and a jigsaw. Prior to operating any power tool you need to read and understand all the operating procedures and safety instructions in the owner's manual. Now let's talk a little about each one of these.

Power Drill

The power drill was the first electric-powered tool. The C&E Fein company created the first portable power drill in Germany in 1895. The drill was heavy and needed two people to operate it, and by today's standards, it was underpowered, but it ruled supreme during its time. About

20 years later, Black & Decker introduced a power drill that was lighter, more powerful, and based on a pistol-grip design that we are familiar with today.

I'm listing the power drill as the only required power tool because of the ease of use and how it speeds up the building process. Of course, you could still accomplish all this with manually operated drills. There are two basic types of hand drills, a ratchet bit brace and a hand crank (also known as an eggbeater). But we will go with the powered version, which there are two kinds available, corded and cordless. I recommend a cordless version, as you're not tethered to the outlet, and with today's battery technology, the difference in power is negligible, especially for our use.

You can find cordless drills on sale for under $50, and they can go up to a few hundred dollars. I would start out with the cheaper ones, as the more expensive ones, which are usually marketed as professional-grade, are designed more for daily use. You can always upgrade later, and then you will have a backup. In fact, I typically use two drills at a time. I will have one with a drill bit in it and the other with a screwdriver bit; that way, you don't have to change out the bits.

Circular Saw

Now to the nice-to-have power tools, both of them are saws. The first is the circular saw. The circular saw has a round saw blade (similar to what you would see on a table saw) that rotates at a high rate of speed; on the perimeter of the saw blade are the cutting teeth made from hardened steel or tungsten carbide. The size of the saw blade can range from as small as 4" to 10"; however, the majority of circular saws are designed for a 7" – 8" saw blade (read the owner's manual of your saw to determine the proper sized saw blade). The size of the saw blade will be the determining factor as to the thickness of material the saw can cut.

A circular saw is designed to make straight cuts while being pushed on the top of the material being cut; the saw blade protrudes from the bottom of the saw. As you push the saw, the rotating saw blade cuts the material. The cutting depth of the saw blade is adjustable, as you only want about a ¼" of the saw blade protruding through the material being cut. The base of the saw can also be tilted, allowing you to make beveled and angled cuts. Although I say a circular is a nice to have tool, it is almost a requirement for some of the projects, so it is a highly recommended nice-to-have tool.

Jigsaw

Unlike the circular saw, which is designed to make straight cuts, the jigsaw is designed to make irregular curved cuts. The jigsaw's saw blade is straight and narrow, allowing it to cut curved shapes. The action of the saw blade is reciprocating in that the saw blade moves up and down. Some jigsaws also have controls that allow the saw blade to move back and forth while also moving up and down. Due to some issues, such as the small size of the saw blade and it not being supported at the bottom, jigsaws can have a control issue; it is easy to get off course of the intended cutting path. When using a jigsaw freehand, a good rule is to cut a little bit outside of the layout lines and sand the material to the line.

When it comes to powering both the circular saw and jigsaw, you have corded or cordless options. The cost of any corded tool will be less than a cordless version, so the choice is up to you, but unlike the drill, I recommend the corded version for your first purchase. If you do purchase any corded tools, don't forget about a good quality extension cord. The main cost of cordless tools is the battery. Suppose you want to start investing in cordless tools. In that case, buy one or two tools that come with batteries and then purchase other cordless tools without the battery, as the batteries are interchangeable (this, of course applies only to the same brand, as a Dewalt battery won't work in a Milwaukee tool, and vice versa).

If you happen to have other power tools, I am not saying that they can't be used, as I am all for getting the job done as easily as possible, but I also want to emphasize that you don't need power tools to create some very nice wood projects. I understand that not everyone who reads this book is a true beginner, but I've created this book for first-time woodworkers in developing basic woodworking skills. So, if you're a master woodworker, just bear with me.

Chapter 5
Joinery

Woodworking can be defined as just a series of techniques. When you understand these techniques and can perform them reasonably well, you can build almost anything. Notice I did not say once you "master" techniques, as it can take years of daily woodworking experience to master many techniques. As a woodworker for over 15 years, I can effectively perform many techniques but still only consider myself a knowledgeable woodworking hobbyist.

One of the most fundamental techniques in woodworking is joinery. Joinery is the act of taking two or more pieces of wood and attaching them to make one item. There are many techniques in accomplishing this and many factors as to what specific technique should be used in a particular project. The two most significant factors in what technique should be used are the available tools and the skill level of the woodworker. It would be unrealistic to demonstrate and expect a novice woodworker to cut a dovetail joint by hand. Let's start with the very basics and work from there.

Before we get into the different joinery techniques, we need to discuss how the joints will be held together. No matter the joint, they all have one thing in common, you want them to be tight. A joint is tight when there are no gaps between the adjoining pieces. There are very few occasions when I don't glue a joint, and if there are any gaps, the glue won't effectively bond the pieces together.

Glues

There are many different kinds of glues that can be used in woodworking; we will discuss a few of them. But regardless of the type of glue, it needs something to bond to. Why is this basic knowledge essential? Let's go back to the straws in representing the biological makeup of wood; how much surface area is there at the ends of the straws compared to the sides? The answer, very little. Since the end grain has substantially less surface area than the long-grain area, it will result in a much weaker bond. One thing that can be done to improve the surface area of end grain is to put some glue on the surface of the end grain, spread it out and let it seep into the wood, then let the glue dry for a few minutes; we want the glue to start bonding with the sides of the wood cells just beneath the surface but still be tacky. Now add more glue (again, spread it out) and connect it to the other piece. This will create a much stronger bond than if you were to just put a layer of glue on and join the pieces. This technique only applies when using wood glue (which is the majority of the time). Now let's talk about the different glues available.

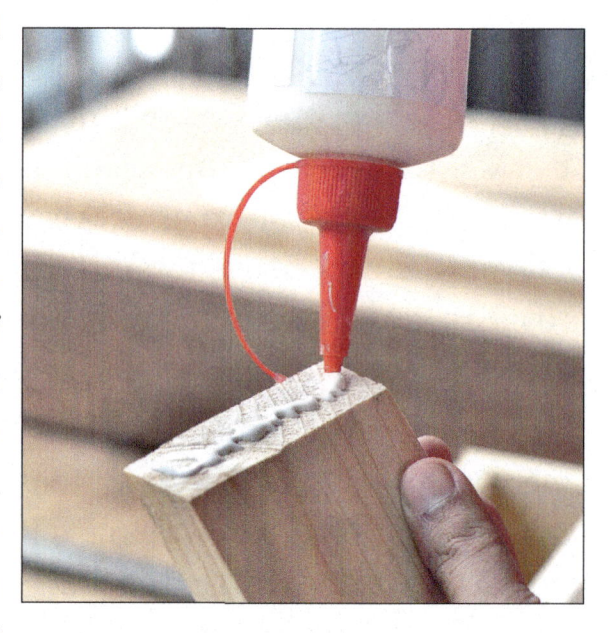

Wood Glue

The technical name of what we call wood glue is polyvinyl acetate; it is also referred to as PVA glue. PVA glue was first developed about 100 years ago and has continuously been improved. The strength of the bond in today's PVA glue is much stronger than the glue from even 30 or 40 years ago. As already mentioned, to achieve a strong bond, the joint needs to be tight, the wood also needs to be dry (PVA glue will not bond well or at all to green lumber), and the joint needs moderate clamping pressure. When correctly done, the glue joint is actually stronger than the surrounding wood; if you were to break a cured PVA glued joint, the surrounding wood fibers would break before the glue bond.

It is also important to understand the difference between glue drying and curing. It can take as short as an hour for PVA glue to dry, but the full bonding strength of the glue won't be achieved until the glue cures, which takes about 24 hours. Another thing to be aware of is that most PVA glues won't cure properly in temperatures below 55 degrees Fahrenheit. Also, if you're planning on staining your project, PVA glue will not accept stains, so you need to make sure all the glue squeeze-out has been removed.

Some PVA glues on the market are water-resistant or waterproof; this means they will hold their bond in wet environments once cured, however the wood still needs to be dry when assembled. Titebond III is an example of a waterproof PVA glue. It is an excellent PVA glue for making cutting boards or any project that will primarily stay outside.

We will be building our projects using PVA glue.

Hide Glue

As the name suggests, this glue is made from animal hides. Before the development of PVA glue, hide glue was the glue used in all woodworking. Conventional hide glue is only available in either solid crystals or pellets, and they need to be heated to become liquid; there are special pots designed just for this purpose. Titebond now makes a hide glue that is already in liquid form. The main woodworking niche that still predominately uses hide glue is guitar making. Even once cured, hide glue can be heated and the joint taken apart without damaging the surrounding wood; this makes any repairs that may be needed years down the road possible.

Other Glues Of Note

I want to mention some other available glues; each one has a purpose in the woodshop. The first is polyurethane glue, a lot of people call this Gorilla glue, but that is a brand name; polyurethane glue has been around a lot longer. Then we have super glue, its real name is cyanoacrylate glue or just CA glue. Next is epoxy, of which there are many different types. Epoxy can be used to fill in voids and can be colored. And last is contact cement, one of the many uses of contact cement is in applying veneers.

Clamps

Ask any woodworker how many clamps you should have, and they will answer something like this – "there is no such thing as too many clamps; you will always need more." There are very few (if any) projects you can build that you won't need at least one (or ten) clamps. There are many types of clamps available; we will discuss the four most used in a woodshop. They are bar clamps, squeeze clamps, pipe clamps, and spring clamps.

Bar Clamps

Bar clamps are so-called because their clamping heads are mounted on a steel bar. One head is usually stationary, while the other head can slide to any position along the bar. The movable head has a screw with a handle that is screwed down to apply the clamping pressure. Bar clamps are by

Chapter 5 - Joinery

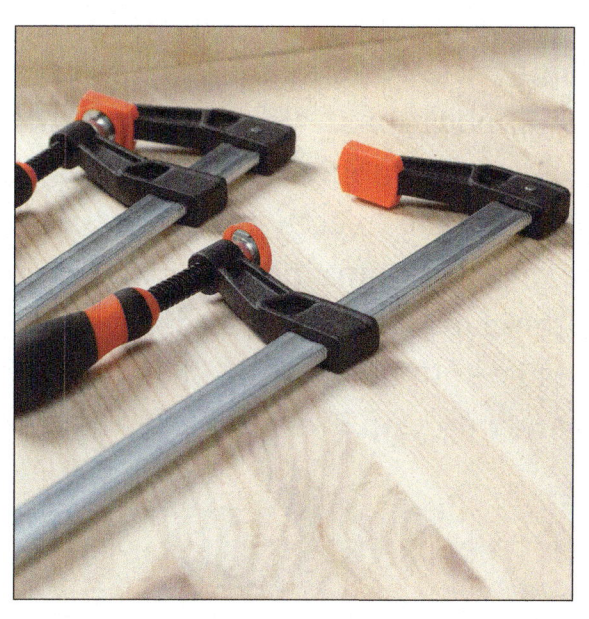

far the most used type of clamp in the woodshop, and there are a few varieties of bar clamps. F-clamps (so named because they resemble the letter "F") are the most widely used type of clamp as they provide more than adequate clamping pressure and are relatively inexpensive. An excellent place to get decent F-clamps is Harbor Freight; they are by far the cheapest I have found. I recommend getting a few of each size, starting with 6" and going up to 18" or 24". Another type of bar clamp that you may want to acquire once you venture into larger projects are parallel clamps, the bars on these clamps are much thicker, and because of this, they are available in longer lengths, but they are also more expensive, starting at around $40 each.

Squeeze Clamps

I listed squeeze clamps as a separate category, although they are a type of bar clamp. They are so-called squeeze clamps because they have a grip that you squeeze to apply clamping pressure. One of the most significant advantages squeeze clamps have over other bar clamps is they can be operated with one hand, while F-clamps and parallel clamps require the use of both hands. With this advantage comes the disadvantage that they do not apply the same clamping pressure, but the pressure is adequate for most applications. When I want more clamping pressure than the squeeze clamp can apply, I will temporarily clamp the pieces together with a squeeze clamp since you can operate the clamp with one hand, and once I have both hands free, I'll come back and apply an F-clamp.

Pipe Clamps

Pipe clamps are very versatile when it comes to length, as you only purchase the jaws of the clamp and use a standard threaded pipe to separate them. The length of the pipe clamp is only limited by the length of the piece of pipe you have. Pipe clamps are not something you will need right away; they are ideal for gluing up boards for tabletops and cutting boards.

Spring Clamps

Spring clamps are so-called because they use the tension of a spring to apply the clamping pressure. Spring clamps come in many different sizes, some quite

Chapter 5 - Joinery

large, and are best used when dealing with smaller pieces that other clamps are just too big to deal with.

Other Clamps

Many other clamps are available, like C-clamps (which are designed more for metalworking), special corner clamps, strap clamps, etc. Even masking tape or painters' tape can be used as a clamp in certain situations. I will end this section with this, no woodworker has ever uttered the phrase – "I think I have enough clamps."

Different Types Of Joints

As already mentioned, a joint is just how two or more pieces of wood are put together. There are many joinery techniques; we'll start with some basic joints and discuss some more elaborate joints. If you want to be amazed at how complex a joint can be, do an internet search for Japanese wood joints; the skill needed to fashion these joints is simply amazing.

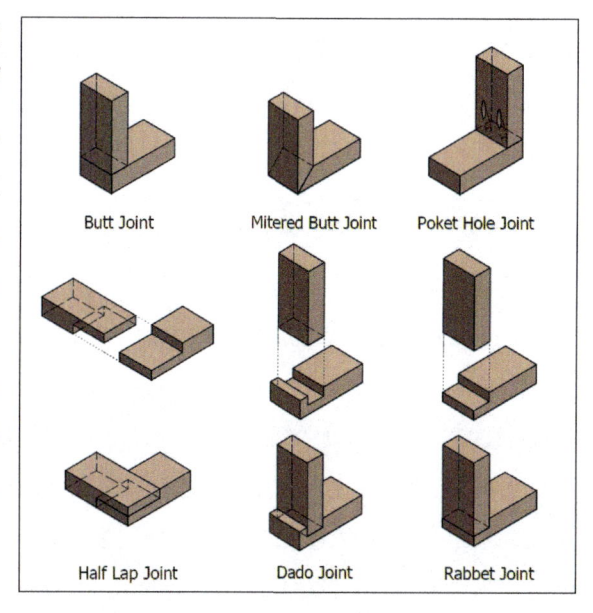

Butt Joint	Mitered Butt Joint	Poket Hole Joint
Half Lap Joint	Dado Joint	Rabbet Joint

Butt Joint

The butt joint is the simplest of joints. Simply put, a butt joint is when one piece of wood is butted up to another, usually at a 90-degree angle, and fastened in place, either with screws or nails. Although this is a relatively weak joint, there are many projects where a butt joint is more than adequate. Adding glue to the joint will significantly increase the strength of the joint, but it will still be structurally weak in that the joint won't be able to withstand much weight or pressure. Most of the projects in this book have butt joints in the construction, but none of the projects are designed to withstand large amounts of weight or pressure.

Mitered Butt Joint

A mitered butt joint, or simply called a mitered joint, is similar to a butt joint, but instead of the pieces being cut at 90-degrees, they are cut at an angle so that the end grain isn't showing, which makes it more aesthetically pleasing to the eye. Most mitered joints are cut at a 45-degree angle, but that is not always the case. This joint is still relatively weak, but you can insert a spline that greatly improves the joint's strength (this will be discussed in future volumes). The majority of picture frames are made using a mitered butt joint.

Pocket Hole Joint

A pocket hole joint is a butt joint that is fastened together with an angled screw. With the addition of the screw, this joint is much stronger than a regular butt joint; add some glue, and you have a relatively strong joint. The thing about pocket holes is you need a jig to drill the holes; there is no way to drill these holes free-handed. There are elaborate pocket hole jigs that cost hundreds of dollars, but there are also simple ones that cost under $20. Another thing about pocket holes is that you must use screws specially designed for pocket holes; you can't use ordinary wood screw.

Half Lap Joint

A half lap joint is when you have two pieces of wood the same thickness, and you remove half the thickness of each piece (the area that is removed has the same dimensions as the piece it will be attached to) so when they are put together, they are flush with each other. A lap joint can produce a lot of long-grain surface area for glue to bond to, resulting in a relatively strong joint when glued. There are many ways to cut a half-lap joint, it can be done on the table saw, with a router, with a circular saw, a hand saw or chiseled out by hand with a chisel.

Dado Joint

A dado joint is a groove cut in one piece of wood that another piece will fit into. A common use for a dado joint is in cabinetry and is most often used when using plywood. There are a couple of ways to cut a dado effectively; the quickest and easiest is with a table saw using a stacked dado saw blade, and another is using a router (this will be discussed further in future volumes).

Rabbet Joint

A rabbet joint is basically a dado that is cut along the edge of a board. Like the dado, this is a common joinery technique used in cabinetry. The joint provides a recessed area on the back of a cabinet for a back panel to be placed so the end grain of the panel won't be seen; it also provides rigidity to the cabinet.

There are many other types of joints, and some of them will be discussed in future volumes. Here are some; tongue and groove, mortise and tenon, biscuit (not the type you eat), dovetail, and box or finger joint.

Beginners Guide To Woodworking

Chapter 6
Finishing The Project

The finishing of a project can be defined as the sanding, staining (if desired), and applying a finish or topcoat. Depending on the project, these steps could make the difference between a project that you're proud to show off or something that needs to go in the fire pit. The first step of the finishing process is the most crucial and often the most neglected – sanding. What the project is can be a determining factor in whether or not to stain the project, as you wouldn't want to stain a cutting board. Other than that, staining a project comes down to personal preference. I won't say I never stain a project, but most of my projects are not stained. To achieve different colors, I will usually use different woods for the color. For a light color, I may use maple, or if I'm looking for a darker look, I may choose walnut. The same can be said of the topcoat. What the project is may dictate the type of final finish used. Again, with the cutting board example, a polyurethane would not be a good choice, mineral oil, or a butcherblock oil would be a much better choice. Now let's get to the details of each of these.

Sanding

As I mentioned, sanding is the most crucial part of the finishing process. You wouldn't think so, but how a piece is sanded will directly impact the final appearance of the piece. But what exactly is sanding? For our purpose, sanding can be defined as the removal of imperfections in wood by gently rubbing the wood with an abrasive material, sandpaper. Three elements in that definition need to be discussed: what is sandpaper, what is meant by gently rubbing, and what is meant by the removal of imperfections.

First, what exactly is sandpaper. Sandpaper is a sheet made up of coarse abrasive materials, either a natural material such as garnet or a synthetic material such as aluminum oxide, these are glued to a backing. The backing is usually made up of either paper or woven fibers. The majority of sandpaper made for hand sanding wood utilizes a paper backing, while sandpaper for power sanders is made with a woven backing. The coarseness of the sandpaper is determined by the size of the abrasive material and is referred to as the grit and is represented by a number, with the lower the number, the rougher the sandpaper. The lowest grit sandpaper I have seen is 24 grit, it looked like little pebbles glued to the paper, which is entirely too coarse for sanding wood, the lowest grit that should be used on wood is 60 grit, and for most softwoods, that is even too low, I usually don't go below 80 grit. The grit range that is recommended for sanding bare wood is 60 to 220 grit.

Chapter 6 - Finishing The Project

Let's talk a bit about how to progress through the different grits and why. In answering this, we first need to define what is meant by "removal of imperfections" within our definition of sanding. You would be hard-pressed to find a piece of wood that doesn't have some imperfections in it, it's these imperfections that gives a piece of wood its character. Next, we need to ask ourselves how much of this character do we want to display in the final piece. If it's a fine piece of furniture, we probably want as few imperfections as possible, while we may want to highlight these imperfections in a rustic farmhouse table. Determining how we will sand a piece depends on what look we're striving for in the final piece. You kind of have to do a little reverse engineering.

If you want a nice smooth board, sanding with 220 grit will achieve that, but it would probably take forever if you started out sanding with 220 grit. You want to start with the lowest grit that will achieve the results you're looking for. This all starts at the beginning when we're choosing the wood for our project, remembering that we need to have an idea of the look we're looking for in the final outcome. If you want very little imperfections try to start with wood that has already been surfaced. Don't start out with rough sawn lumber unless you have the equipment to surface it yourself. Now, if you want a very rustic look, rough-sawn wood with a lot of knots in it may be just what you're looking for.

So you decided on a nice smooth finished project with little to no imperfections and started the project with surfaced wood. Even surfaced lumber may still have some saw marks on it, and we will want to get rid of them. But now we also need to consider what type of wood we are going to use. Will it be a softwood or hardwood? If it's a softwood, we may want to start sanding with 100 grit, if it's a hardwood 80 grit may be a better starting point. If the wood is already smooth with no saw marks, we might start with 120 grit for the softwood and 100 grit for the hardwood.

Next, you sit down and get comfortable to start sanding. You pull out a sheet of sandpaper to get to work. A full sheet of sandpaper is usually 9" x 11". It's usually not practical to use the whole sheet at once. What I typically do is cut it into strips, and then I fold the strips in thirds. There is no die-hard rule on how to break down a sheet of sandpaper. Do some experimentation and find what works best for you. Whatever you decide to do, I don't think the sandpaper police will be coming after you.

Before you actually start sanding, it's important to know that there is a correct way to sand and an incorrect way. Even if you've never been in a woodshop before, there is a better than average chance that you've heard the phrase to "sand with the grain." And that would be the correct way of sanding. Also, long strokes are better than short strokes. Sanding against the grain is not the only thing you don't want to do, but you also don't want to sand in circular motions.

Now you actually start sanding. You're using pine for the project, which has very few saw marks, so you start with 120 grit sandpaper. But the saw marks don't seem to be going away, so you start sanding faster and start putting some elbow

Chapter 6 - Finishing The Project

grease into it. STOP! If you're putting too much effort into sanding, you need to go down in grit, let the sandpaper do the work, as the definition said, "gently rubbing." Using elbow grease is the opposite of "gently." You go down to 100 grit, and the saw marks go away, and you didn't need to grease up your elbow. You finish sanding the entire piece with 100 grit sandpaper, and 99% of the imperfections are gone. This first course of sanding with the lowest grit sandpaper is where all the work is done in achieving the final look.

The issue now is that the coarse sandpaper you used left behind many scratch marks, and you planned on staining the project. All those scratch marks will be highlighted as the stain is absorbed by them like a dry sponge. This is why you continue sanding with finer grit sandpaper. As I said, the first course does the job; the subsequent courses are only to remove the scratch marks left by the last course. The rule here is that the grit of the following course should be no more than 1.5 times that of the previous course. For our example, we used 100 grit, so the subsequent sanding should not be above 150 grit. Of course, you could go lower, let's say to only 120 grit. If the second sanding was done at 150 grit, then the third sanding could go to our target grit of 220, as 1.5 of 150 is 225. But if our second sanding was only to 120 grit, then the highest we could go with the third sanding is 180 grit, and then we would need a fourth sanding to finish at our target grit of 220.

I hope this makes sense to you, but we ain't done yet. A question that always comes up is, why stop at 220 grit? If we went to 320 grit or even 400 grit, wouldn't it make it even smoother? The answer is yes, it would make it smoother, BUT. There is always a "BUT" in there. The issue is when you start going beyond 220 grit, you are no longer sanding the wood, but you are now polishing the wood. In essence, you are filling in the wood pores and making the wood as slick as a piece of glass, which will affect the way stain is absorbed. It can also make the wood so slick that finishes, such as polyurethane, shellac, lacquer, etc., won't have anything to grab on to and could flake off.

Now you're asking if we are finally done? Not entirely, there is one more thing to talk about. If you plan on painting the project, there is no reason to go beyond 150 grit. Compared to stains and finishes, paint is extremely thick and needs something substantial to grab onto, and sanding beyond 150 dramatically reduces the amount of material available for the paint to adhere to. We'll finish this section with this. Sanding is more of an art form. There are no set-in-stone recipes or formulas to follow. It's kind of like bar-b-queuing, everyone has their own way of doing it and will argue tooth and nail that their way is the best way. The only thing that can be agreed on is low temperature for a long time (low and slow). The only thing that is agreed on with sanding is that it is the most important part of a good finish. There are entire books out there just on sanding.

Wood Stains

Now let's talk about wood stains. The first question is, what is a wood stain? A wood stain is a solvent with either dyes or pigments added to give it color. Wood stains are translucent, which allows the natural grain of the wood to show through. There are many different types of wood stains. We will be concentrating on three of them; Oil-based stain, water-based stain, and gel stain.

Chapter 6 - Finishing The Project

Regardless of the type of stain used, the wood must be properly prepped to receive the stain. Most of this prep work has already been completed with proper sanding, but more needs to be done. Other than gel stains, most stains are very thin, almost the consistency of water, and will penetrate the wood fibers. Being a natural material, wood fibers are not uniform, so the stain will be absorbed differently within the same piece of wood, which could result in a splotchy appearance. To help reduce this, we need to prepare the wood to receive the stain by applying a pre-stain wood conditioner. Just as stains are either water-based or oil-based, so are conditioners, and you can't mix them up, as oil and water won't mix. When it comes to the end grain, which is highly porous, ensure a thick coat of conditioner is applied. Ensure you read the directions on the can, as the procedures can differ from product to product. Also, when using water-based products, the water will be absorbed by the wood fibers and swell, so a light sanding may be required after the conditioner dries.

Let's talk about the stains. Oil-based stains come in a variety of wood-toned colors, while water-based stains can be tinted to hundreds of different colors. Just that alone may be the deciding factor of which type of stain to use. Water-based stains dry faster than oil-based stains, and water-based stains clean up with soap and water. Oil-based stains tend to have more of a natural look. There is no right or wrong answer on which type of stain to use. The best thing to do is make some tests on scrap wood. Just be sure to use the same kind of wood. If your project is made of pine, don't do your tests on oak.

There are a few different ways to apply stain; using a bristle brush, foam brush, or rag. You can use any of these methods with any stain, although each stain will have recommendations for applying. Whatever you use to apply the stain, always apply it with the grain. Stain is different than paint. Paint adheres to the surface of the wood while stain penetrates the wood. So once you've applied the stain, you need to wipe off the excess. If you want a darker result, you won't succeed by putting on a thicker coat as you will be wiping off the excess anyway. Wait an hour or so and apply another coat.

When it comes to putting a topcoat over stain, if you are using an oil-based stain, you can use either an oil-based or water-based topcoat. On the other hand, if you use a water-based stain, you need to use a water-based topcoat. Before you apply any topcoat, you need to let the stain fully dry. For some oil-based stains, this can be as long as 24 hours, while water-based stains will usually only take 2-3 hours.

Top-Coats

There are too many finishers available that it would be impossible to list them all, as some will undoubtedly be missed. Here is a shortlist: polyurethane, shellac, lacquer, boiled linseed oil, mineral oil, beeswax, etc. Even in this very short list, did any of them surprise you? Many factors come into play when deciding on what finish to use. This includes the wood used in building the project, was it stained, what is its purpose, will it be in a humid environment? The majority of woodworking hobbyists tend to use a polyurethane of some kind, as these are readily available and relatively easy to apply.

Polyurethane

As with stains, polyurethane is either oil-based or water-based. Like stain, oil-based polyurethanes take longer to dry than water-based. In the can, oil-based polyurethanes have an amber color and will maintain a slight amber sheen after being applied and will darken over time. Water-based polyurethane is milky in color in the can but dries completely clear. As mentioned earlier, water-based polyurethane can be applied to wood that has been stained with either water-based or oil-based stain, but oil-based polyurethane cannot be used on wood that has been stained with a water-based stain; a water-based polyurethane must be used. Don't apply any finish to wood that has been stained until the stain has completely dried (which can be up to 24 hours for oil-based stains); the solvent in the polyurethane can activate the damp stain and pull the stain out of the wood.

Most polyurethanes need to be applied using a bristle brush. The exception is wipe-on polyurethane which is applied with a cloth. Wipe-on polyurethane is usually an oil-based polyurethane that's been diluted with mineral spirits (don't get mineral spirits confused with mineral oil). You can make your own wipe-on polyurethane for a fraction of the cost of a premixed wipe-on. The ratio when mixing is 50-75% polyurethane, then the remaining 25-50% mineral spirits. Do some experimentation as to what is best for you. The wipe-on polyurethane I use most of the time is a 65/35 mix (65% polyurethane/35% mineral spirits). For the best finish, apply polyurethane in thin coats, most of the time three coats will be enough when using full-strength polyurethane. Since wipe-on polyurethane has been diluted, it may require as many as four or five coats. No matter what kind of polyurethane you use, it should be applied with the grain of the wood.

All polyurethanes need to be mixed as the polymers and solvent will separate. Mixing needs to be done by stirring. Do not shake polyurethane as this will create air bubbles that will be noticeable in the dried finish. You can however, gently shake wipe-on polyurethane since it has been thinned with mineral spirits, any bubbles that do form will dissipate quickly.

Did I mention polyurethane comes in different sheens? Most oil-based polyurethanes are available in gloss, semi-gloss, and satin sheens, while water-based polyurethanes are available in those sheens plus matte and ultra-flat.

Food Safe Finishers

It is important to understand what kind of finishers are safe for items that will come in contact with food, such as cutting boards or our taco shell holder. The most widely used food-safe finish is mineral oil. Products such as butcher block oil or cutting board oil usually have a mineral oil base with other ingredients that help protect the wood that are also food safe. With

Chapter 6 - Finishing The Project

projects like this we want to protect the wood, but we don't want to seal it. It also needs to be understood that these finishes are not a one-time affair, the item needs to be periodically treated to prevent the wood from becoming dry and brittle. The finish also prevents liquids from penetrating the wood and becoming a breeding ground for germs and bacteria. What you don't want to use as a finish for food handling items is any kind of cooking oil, as these oils can become rancid and a breeding ground for bacteria. Beeswax is another good food-safe finish that is widely used on cutting boards.

Here is some trivia you may not know, shellac is an all-natural polymer that is extensively used to coat certain foods. Many candies have a coating of shellac on them.

Beginners Guide To Woodworking

Chapter 7
Woodworking Plans

Now it's time to start having fun, it's finally time to start making some saw dust.

So far in this book we've talked about different tools, techniques, and applications. Which are all vital in developing your skill, now we get to put that knowledge into practice. The majority of skill development is done when actually performing that skill. I also want to emphasize that the first time you perform any new skill you're probably not going to be very good at it, but I don't want you to get discouraged, that is all part of the learning process. It takes time to effectively perform new skills.

Now you might be thinking that these plans are very simplistic, especially if you've done some woodworking in the past, and you would be correct. These plans are designed for the complete beginner in developing the very basic woodworking skills.

When building a project, the first thing we need to do is determine what type of wood will be used in the project, the projects in this book are designed to help you in developing your skills in selecting the right type of wood for different projects. Not only is it important in choosing the type of wood for a project, but it is also important that the dimensions of the wood are adequate so you can layout the pieces to be cut. Efficient use of the wood is not always the best way in laying out your project. An example, if you have a narrow piece in a project and the most efficient use of the wood you have would have the grain running in the narrow direction of the piece, this would make the piece vulnerable to splitting. It would be a much better option to have the grain running along the long length of the piece even if it meant you needed to waste some wood in order to make the cut.

When drawing a layout line there is an inside and outside to that line. The area that is inside the line is the piece being cut, while outside the line is what is called the waste, this area is not part of the final piece. When cutting the pieces, the cut should be made on the outside of the layout line, the line should still be visible on the final piece. It is much easier to trim down to the line then it is to reattach wood. Don't worry about the mark left, a little bit of sanding will take care of it.

Choosing what tools to use is also important. Using the proper tool will not only provide the best result it will also prevent a lot of frustration on your part. An overly simplified example is try screwing in a slotted head screw using a Philips head screw driver. As mentioned previously in this book, you need to have an idea of the final look you're looking for. If it is a rustic look you're looking for, you may not care if there are saw marks or even if the cuts aren't 100% straight.

Before getting started on the projects, you're going to need a relatively stable surface to work on. Of course, a good workbench would

Chapter 7 - Woodworking Plans

be the best solution, but if you don't have a good workbench don't fear there are ways to provide an adequate work surface. A very simple remedy is to use a piece of 3/4" plywood between two items. Here I demonstrate this using some plastic sawhorses available at a big box store, but if you don't have any sawhorses, you could use a couple of trash cans or stools or chairs (or any two items that are about the same height). What I would not recommend is using the kitchen table as a workbench. No matter how careful you will be, I guarantee there will be inadvertent cuts into the table at some point (this comes from personal experience).

The first project, which is the bird feeder, will have in-depth instructions. I won't go as in-depth on the other projects as I will refer to the instruction of the bird feeder. Now let's get started cutting some wood.

Beginners Guide To Woodworking

Chapter 7 - Woodworking Plans

Bird Feeder

The bird feeder is by far the best example in demonstrating the importance of proper wood layout. With the two narrow roof supports and the narrow base frame pieces we need to cut these pieces with the grain running length wise. Especially the roof supports which will be used to hang and carry the weight of the feeder.

Since a bird feeder is designed to be outside and a finish will not be applied (birds like unfinished wood better then finished wood to eat and live in), the choice of wood should be of a species that is naturally resistant to rot, the best choices would be cedar, cypress or redwood. Of course you

Beginners Guide To Woodworking

could make it out of pine as it is much cheaper, it just won't last as long. I'm going to be using pine in the demonstration photos.

I designed this bird feeder to be made from one 6 ' long 8" x 1" board that can be purchased at a big box store (the actual dimension of the board is 7 1/2" x 3/4").

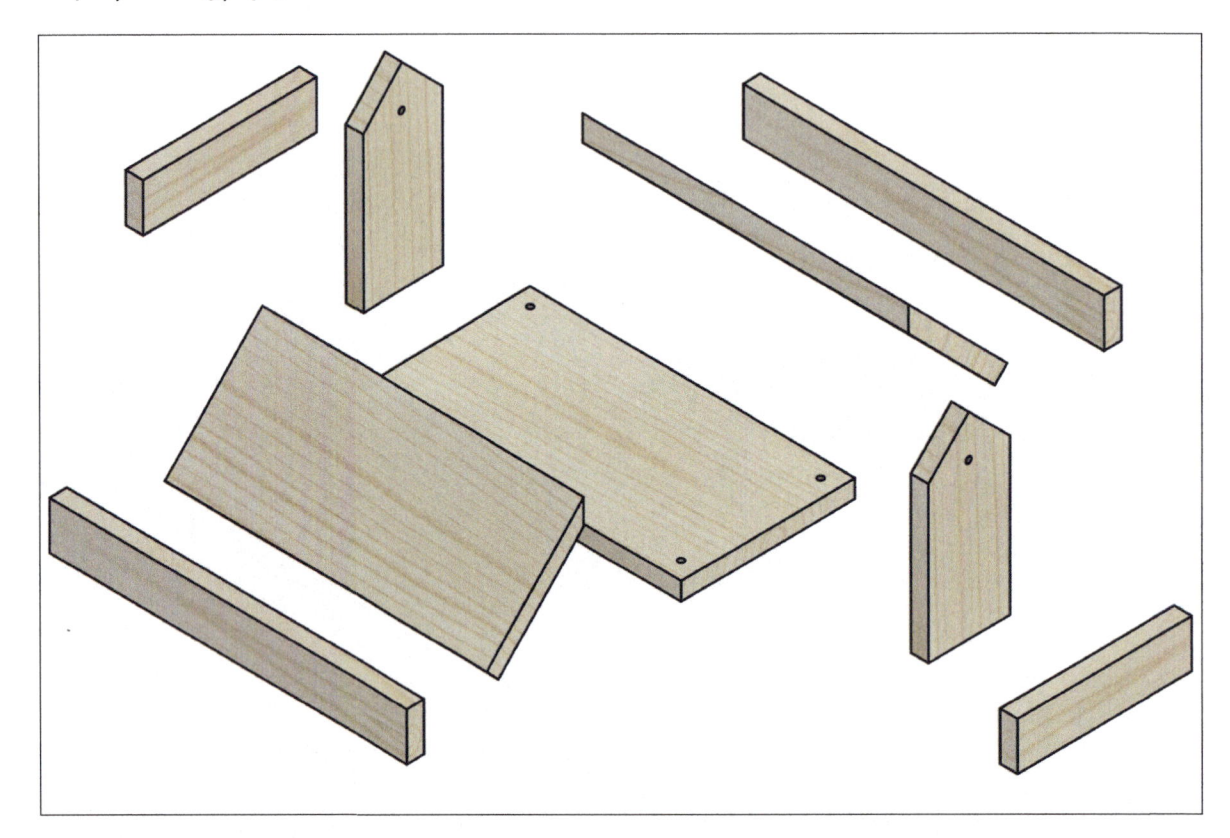

When marking out the layout lines they should not be laid out all out at once, this would result in using the same line for two different pieces, and the kerf of the blade (which has already been covered as the thickness of the saw blade) will make the second piece that much shorter and throw off the measurements. To ensure a piece won't inadvertently be cut short the lay out lines should be drawn for each cut individually. It is also a good idea that wood be purchased oversized by at least 10-20% to ensure you won't run short, if the project calls for a 2' board to cut the pieces from, recommend purchasing one that is at least 2.5'.

Chapter 7 - Woodworking Plans

The first pieces to be laid out are the floor and sides of the base, all of these pieces have 90 degree cuts. The base is pretty straight forward, as the width of the board is the width of the base, it just needs to be cut to length. If using a circular saw to make these cuts, the easiest ways to ensure a straight cut is to use a guide for the base of the saw to ride against as the cut is being made, the speed square is the perfect guide in this situation. Since the boards are 7 1/2" wide a miter box would not be a viable option since most miter boxes only allow for a maximum of 4" wide boards. When making the cut be aware of the kerf the blade will make and measure from the blade to the edge of the base and place the guide that distance from your layout line. If using a hand saw, place the guide on the layout line and put the saw up against the guide, the saw should now be covering up the layout line. Move the guide and saw until the layout line is visible. In either case it is a good idea to clamp the guide to the wood so the guide won't move.

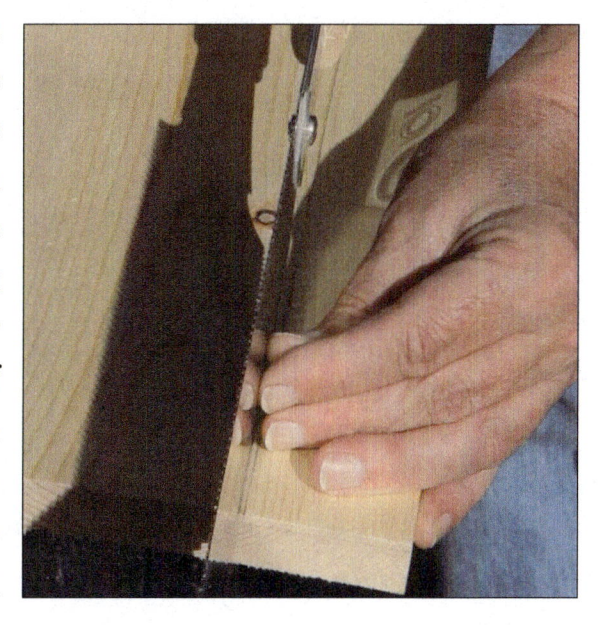

The framing pieces need to be ripped. First cut a piece from the board that is the length of the long frame pieces plus 2 times the thickness of the pieces as these pieces will overlap the base and the two side pieces (add a little more to be on the safe side)(if you're following the plan dimensions this cut should be about 16"). Next rip the pieces to desired width. In ripping the frame pieces, it is not recommended that a circular saw be used, as the pieces are too narrow to do this safely. The combination square is the perfect tool for drawing the layout lines, set the square to the desired depth (plan dimensions are 2"), place the square on the edge of the board and a pencil up against the end of the ruler, then pull the square with the pencil down the length of the board. Using a hand saw rip the pieces following the outside of the layout line as best you can. This will result in 3 pieces being cut. Now cut the pieces to length, 2 of the pieces just need to be trimmed to make the long frame pieces and the third piece will produce the two short frame pieces. Make sure to cut the frame pieces to go around the floor base, not on top of it. The miter box is the perfect tool for cutting the frame pieces to length. Use the base board and two frame pieces to determine how long to cut each piece, lay the piece to be cut against these to make a cut mark. This provides an accurate measurement without using a tape measure or ruler.

The roof supports are cut next. The two roof supports need angled cuts at the top to accommodate the sloped roof. These cuts will be made at 45 degrees. First, is to make the support pieces, this is done in the same manner as the base frame pieces only these are 3 1/2" wide. Once the pieces are cut, layout the angled lines. Mark the center of the width on the end of each piece, since the pieces were cut to a width

Chapter 7 - Woodworking Plans

of 3 1/2", just divide that in half, which is 1 3/4" and measure in from the edge to make a mark. Using the 45 degree angle of either the combination square or speed square draw the layout line from the mark to the edge of the piece. With these pieces being narrow like the base frame pieces, it is advisable to cut these with a hand saw. Again, the miter box is the perfect tool for these angled cuts.

The last pieces to be cut are the roof pieces. First thing is to cut each roof piece from the board, these will be straight 90-degree cuts and each piece will be 14" long (cut them longer if you want the roof to overhang the roof supports). A 45-degree bevel needs to be cut on each piece so that they will meet at the roofs peak. The easiest way to make the beveled cut is to use the circular saw and adjust the base to 45 degrees. Clamp the work piece to a worktable so it won't move around, just make sure there is some scrap wood underneath the work piece so you won't cut into the work table. Use another piece of straight wood and clamp it to the piece as a guide (the speed square won't be long enough for this cut). The 45-degree bevel will be made on a long grain edge, don't make the mistake of cutting the bevel on the end grain edge. When cutting pieces like this by hand (unlike on a table saw), it is easier to make the beveled cut first and then cut the pieces to the desired width.

Now that all the pieces are cut it is time for assembly. All the joints in this build are butt joints. In the demonstration photos I will be assembling it using glue and screws. It could be assembled with just screws or even nails, but adding glue to any of those will greatly increase the strength of the joint. There are many types of screws and nails available, just make sure to use ones that are for external use. The project could also be assembled using only glue; just ensure each joint is clamped for at least 12 hours to allow the glue time to cure. Since this is an outdoor project make sure to use a waterproof glue, an excellent choice would be to use Titebond III. Since most of the joints are in the area of the end grain of the wood it is advisable to predrill holes if assembling using screws or nails or there is a risk that the ends could split.

The order of assembly isn't crucial with this project. There are certain projects that need to be assembled in a particular order or it won't go together at all. Here the base will be assembled first. First thing to do is to predrill for the screws. Since pine is being used, which is a softwood, combined with this being a project for the outdoors, I decided not to countersink the predrilled holes. If a hardwood was being used it would be advisable to counter sink the holes. Just like when cutting the pieces, it is good practice to lay out the locations where to drill for the screws. There will be two screws going into the base and one screw into each side piece.

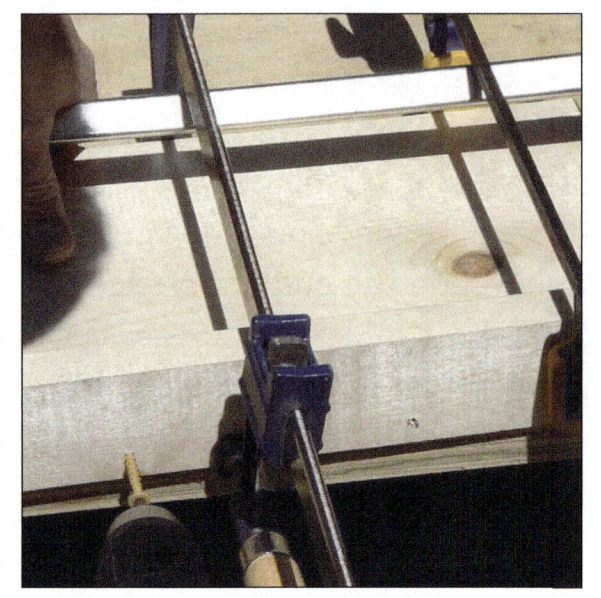

In attaching first long frame piece, first apply glue to the piece and spread it out. Most of the time I will use an acid brush to spread out the glue, but there are times when I will just use that thing attached to my hand called a finger. Don't just apply a bead of glue, always spread the glue out to create a uniformed film, doing this will create a better bond. Ensure enough glue is applied, if there isn't enough glue in the joint the glue won't adhere properly resulting in a weak joint. The telltale sign that enough glue is being used is when the pieces are put together and clamping pressure is applied there should be some glue that squeezes out from the joint. If there is no squeeze out, not enough glue was used and the joint won't be as strong.

Before driving in the screws clamp the pieces together, this will ensure the pieces won't move as the screws are driven in. Also predrill into the base to ensure the base won't split, just drill through the holes already made in the frame piece and drive in the screws. Even after the screws are driven in it is good practice to leave the pieces clamped for at least an hour, this gives the glue some time to set. Remember it may only take an hour or so for the glue to dry, but it will take about 24 hours for the glue to fully cure.

The next pieces to attach are the two shorter side pieces. It is easier to attach these before the other longer piece, this way you won't need to squeeze these pieces in. They will also be attached with glue and screws. Apply the glue, clamp them both against the base as well as against the long piece that has already been attached. Predrill through all the holes again and drive in the screws. There are two screws that go from the short pieces into the base and one screw from the long piece into each of the short pieces.

Now attach the last long piece, just like the other pieces, glue, place, clamp, predrill, and drive in the screws. The base is almost finished, the last thing to do is to drill some drainage holes. These will be 1/4" holes in each corner. That so they will be in the same location in each corner make a template with the location of the hole 1/2" in from each side. The template does two things, first it ensures the hole will be in the same location in each corner and it will also reduce any tear-out. Tear-out is when wood fibers are ripped out when drilling or sawing, leaving jagged edges. Tear-out occurs both where the drill bit enters and exits the wood, although it is usually worse on the exit side. Placing scrap pieces of wood where the drill bit will exit will greatly reduce the amount of tear-out.

Next is to attach the roof supports. The first thing that needs to be done is to drill holes for the rope in order to be able to hang the bird feeder. The size of the hole will depend on the size of the rope used. I'm using 1/4" rope, so least 1/4" holes need to be drilled (it can be a good idea to drill the holes a little larger than the rope). The center of the hole will be 2" down from the peak and centered. Just like when drilling the drainage holes use some scrap wood when drilling to reduce tear-out. Next predrill for the screw to attach the post, this will be about 1" up from the bottom and centered. Just like when attaching the base frame pieces, glue, place, clamp, predrill, and drive in the screw.

Now it's time to put the roof on. Only one screw will be used on each side of each roof piece, predrill about 1 1/2" down from the peak and half the thickness of the roof supports. There is no way to effectively clamp the roof, just apply some glue and drive in the screws. The roof doesn't provide any structural support, so it not being clamped is not a big concern.

Chapter 7 - Woodworking Plans

The last thing to do is to attach the rope to hang the bird feeder. Thread the rope through the hole and tie a knot at the end, repeat on the other support. A little light sanding with 150 grit sandpaper could be done to get rid of any pencil marks. Some screening material can also be placed over the drainage holes to prevent the bird seed from falling through. As has been mentioned before this is your project, make it the way you want it, woodworking plans are just guides.

To view a video of this project being built go to:

https://youtu.be/CL8cpXWzFO4

Part	Qty.	T	W	L	Mat'l	Notes
Base	1	3/4"	7 1/2"	14"	Pine	
Long Frame	2	3/4"	2"	15 1/2"	Pine	
Short Frame	2	3/4"	2"	7 1/2"	Pine	
Roof Support	2	3/4"	3 1/2"	8 1/4"	Pine	45 degree cuts to create roof peak
Roof	2	3/4"	6"	14"	Pine	45 degree bevel cut on long edge
Rope	1					1/4" (use what you want)

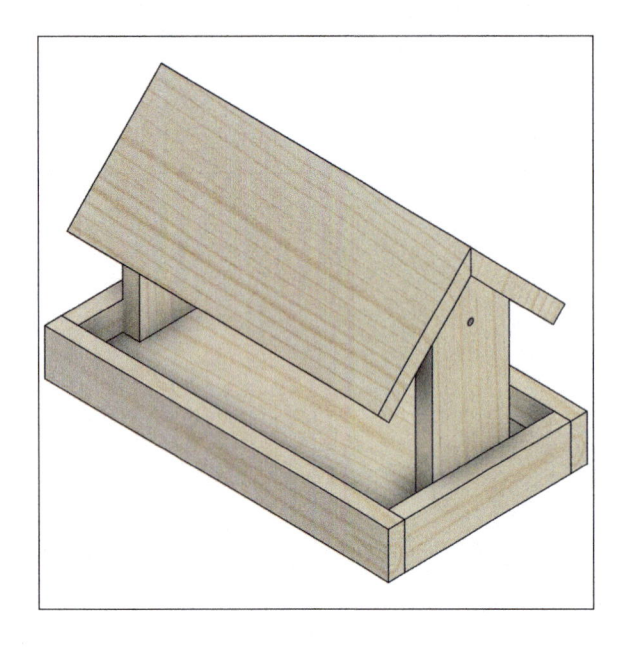

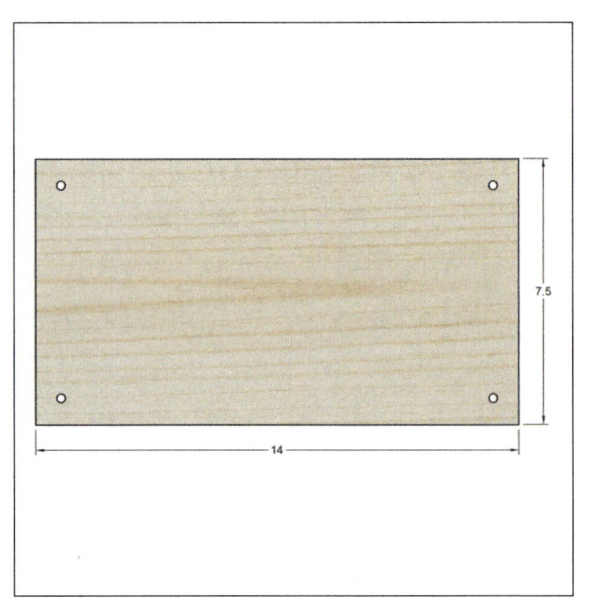

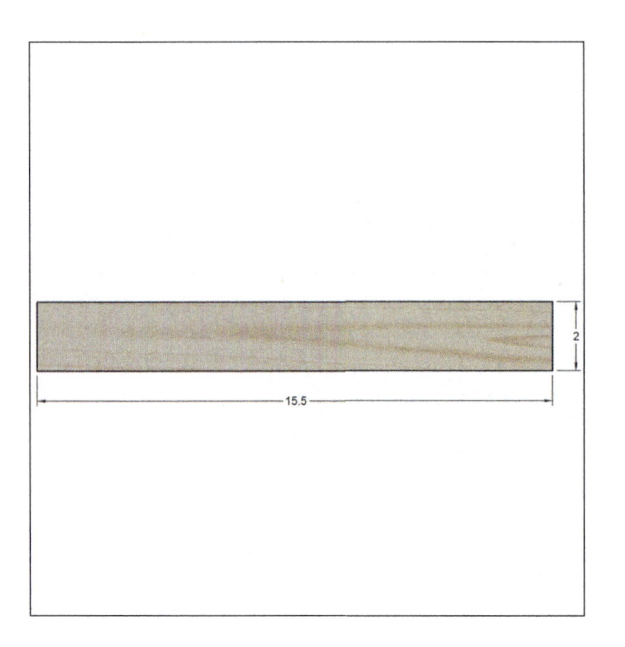

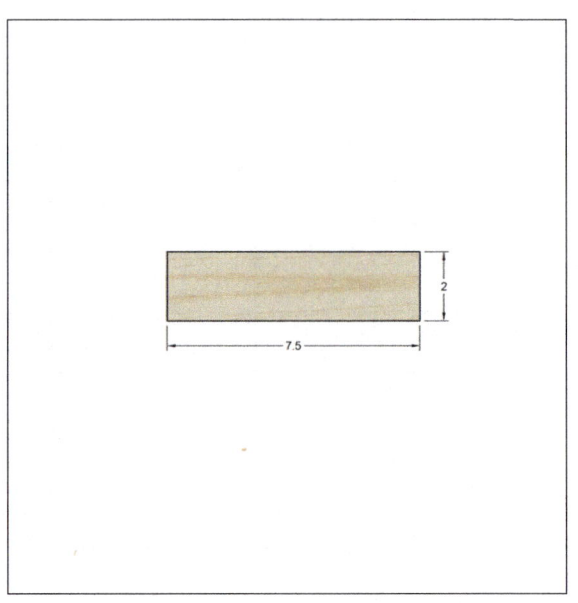

Beginners Guide To Woodworking

80

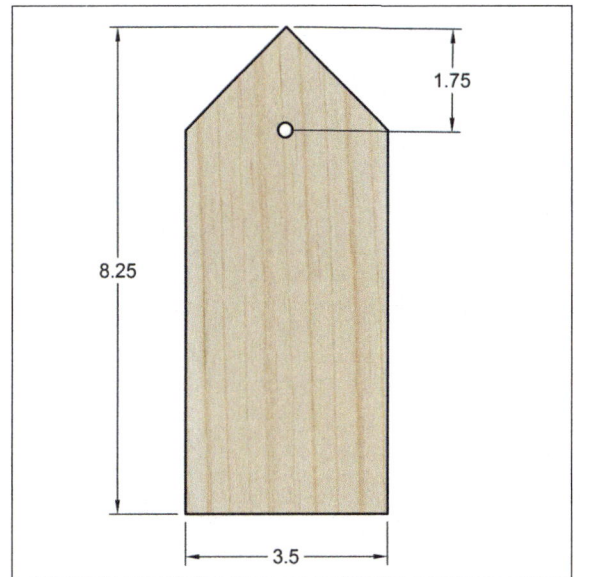

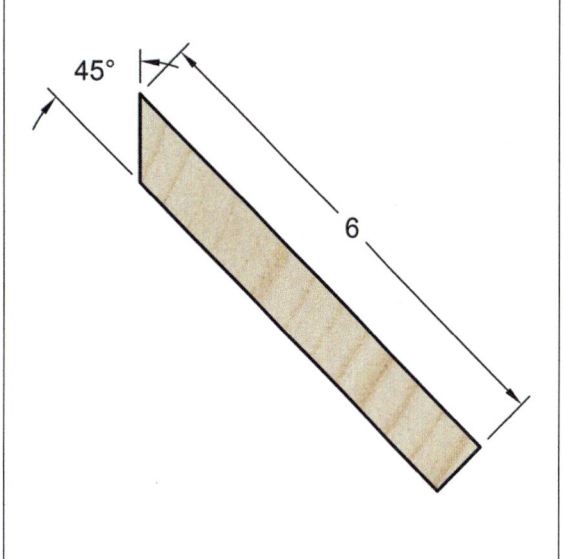

Chapter 7 - Woodworking Plans

Beginners Guide To Woodworking

Chapter 7 - Woodworking Plans

Bird House

Let's give the birds a place to live as well as to eat, it's time to build a bird house. As with the bird feeder building the bird house with naturally rot resistant wood would be ideal, but it can still be made from pine, it just won't last as long. This bird house is designed to be built from one 6' long 6" x 1" board (again, the actual dimensions would be 5 1/2" x 3/4").

A little about bird houses, the size of the house and of the access hole will determine what species of bird will call it home. You may see many bird houses with perches under the hole, I don't put a perch there as it provides a place for predators to sit and steal the eggs.

Beginners Guide To Woodworking

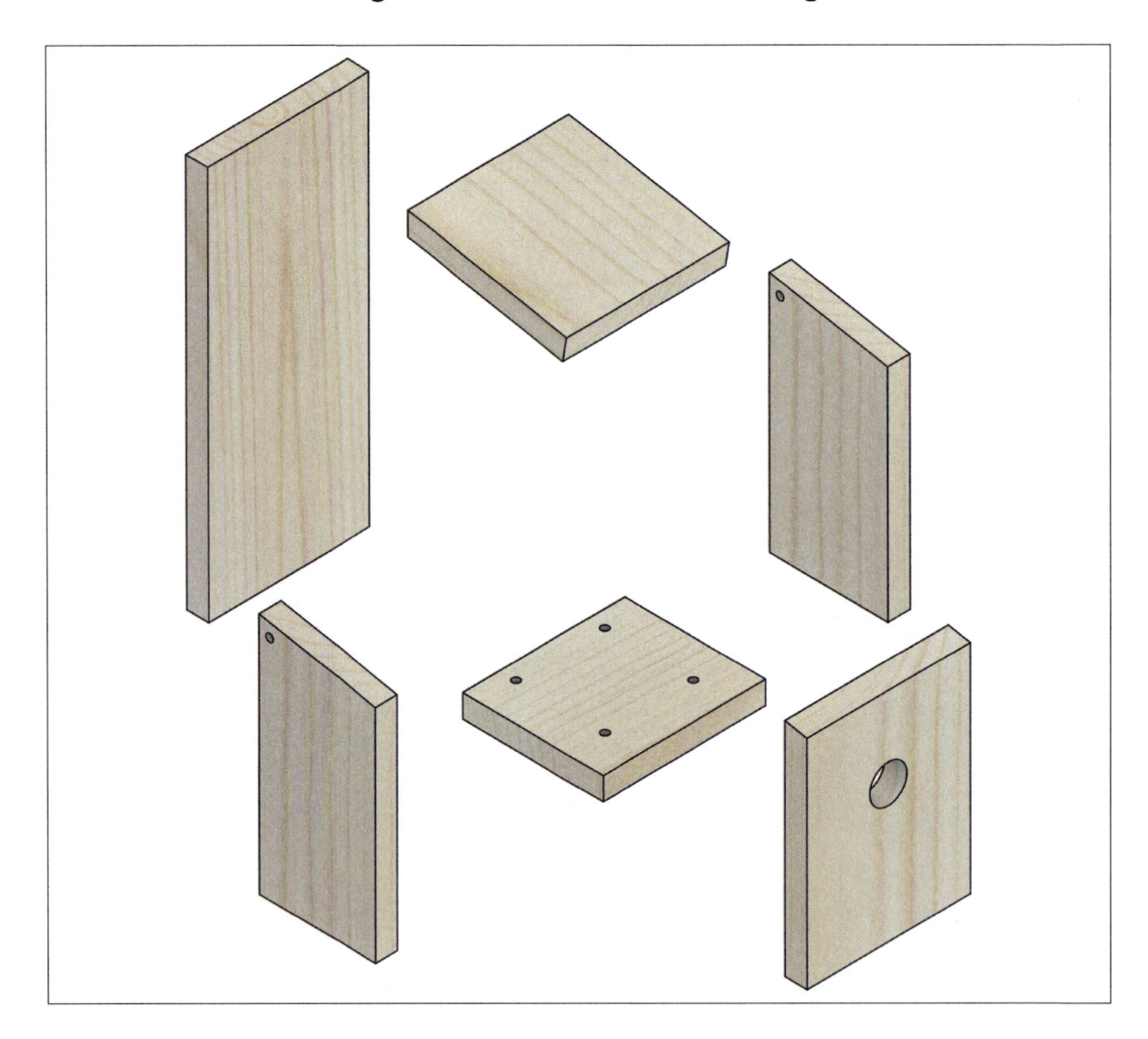

Refer to the bird feeder for details on how to layout and cut the pieces.

Let's cut the pieces first. As I've said many times, woodworking plans are just guides, it is your project, and you can build it to any dimension you want. You can follow the dimensions listed in the drawing if you wish, as I will be making my cuts according to the drawing.

There are two pieces that need to be cut that don't have 90-degree cuts, the top of the two sides are cut 10-degrees from 90-degrees. Use a protractor to layout these lines. These pieces are wider than the roof supports of the

Chapter 7 - Woodworking Plans

bird feeder and can safely be cut with a circular saw. There are also two pieces, the roof and the front piece, that need a 10-degree bevel cut.

Just as with the bird feeder, the bird house will be assembled using glue and screws. The first pieces to be putting together are the back and floor. A bird house needs drainage, so some 1/4" holes will be drilled in the floor piece prior to assembly. Ensure to account for the side pieces that will go on the floor when drilling these holes. Clamping a speed square after assembly and before the glue dries will help ensure that the floor and back will be at a perfect 90-degrees.

Next is to attach the sides. Predrill holes for the screws in the floor and back. The top of the sides have 10-degree angle, ensure the higher part is up against the back. A bird house also needs some ventilation, this can be achieved by drilling a hole on each side. Some bird houses may either have the roof or a side on hinges, this is done to allow for the bird house to be cleaned out once its tenant has departed, I don't believe this is necessary as a new tenant will clean it out when they move in. But this is your bird house, if you want to be able to clean it out, by all means attach a side using a hinge.

Predrill the front piece to attach it. A hole needs to be drilled in the front to allow birds to get in and out. The front has the 10-degree beveled cut on the top, ensure the high point of the bevel is up against the side pieces. The angle of the side pieces and the bevel of the front piece should be in line with each other. When cutting the front, it is best to make the beveled cut first and then cut it to length.

Beginners Guide To Woodworking

The roof is the last piece to attach. Predrill for the screws and attach with the beveled cut up against the back. This bird house is designed with the back extending past the roof in order to allow it to be mounted to a pole or tree.

Painting or finishing the outside of the bird house is an option, but do not finish the inside, as mentioned earlier, birds like unfinished houses.

To view a video of this project being built go to:

https://youtu.be/XZ2Zv-EgN6o

Part	Qty.	T	W	L	Mat'l	Notes
Back	1	3/4"	5 1/2"	13"	Pine	
Floor	1	3/4"	5 1/2"	4 3/4"	Pine	
Side	2	3/4"	4"	8"	Pine	10 degree cut on top for roof slope
Front	1	3/4"	5 1/2"	7 1/3"	Pine	10 degree bevel cut on top edge
Roof	1	3/4"	5 1/2"	5 1/2"	Pine	10 degree bevel cut on back edge

Chapter 7 - Woodworking Plans

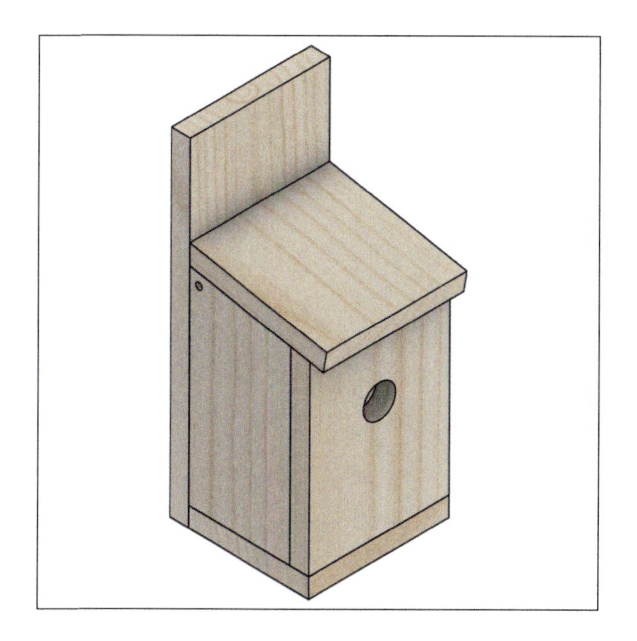

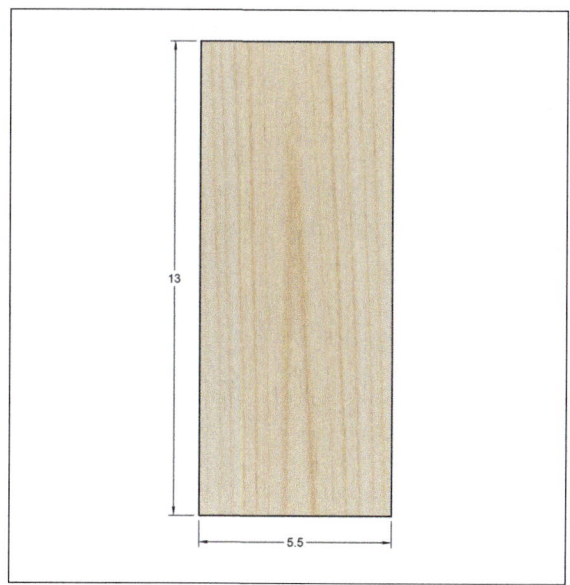

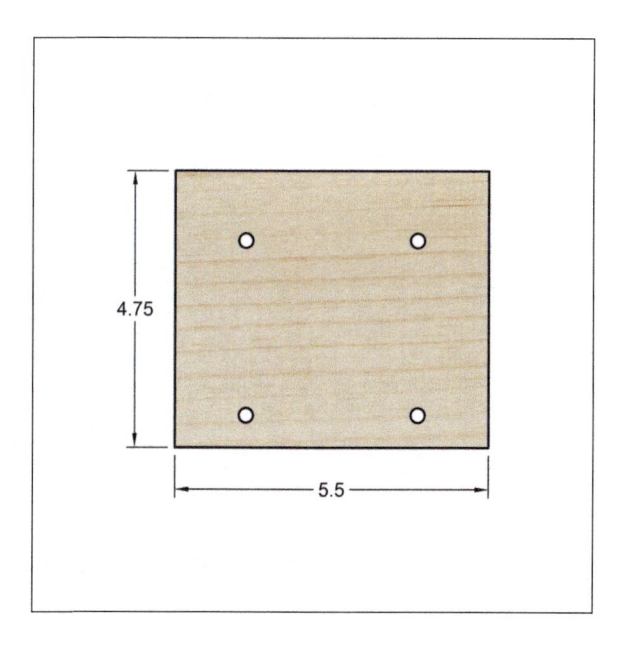

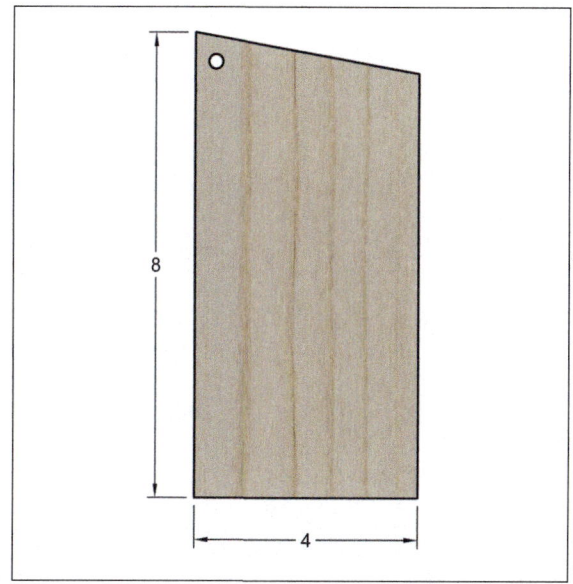

87

Beginners Guide To Woodworking

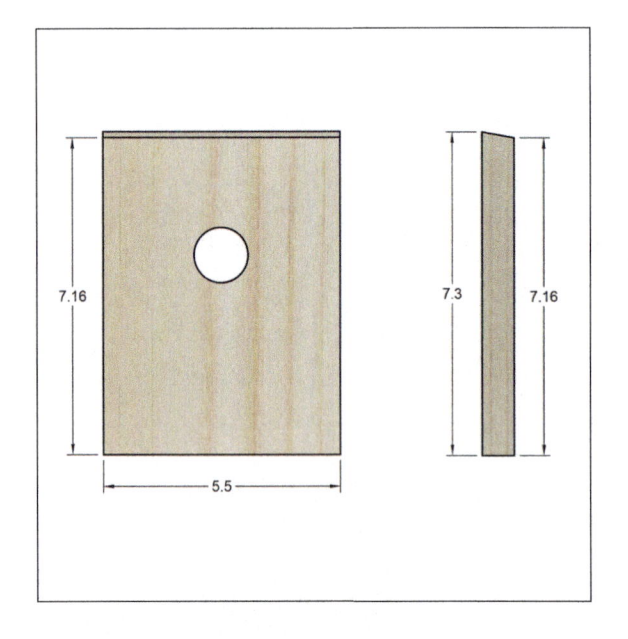

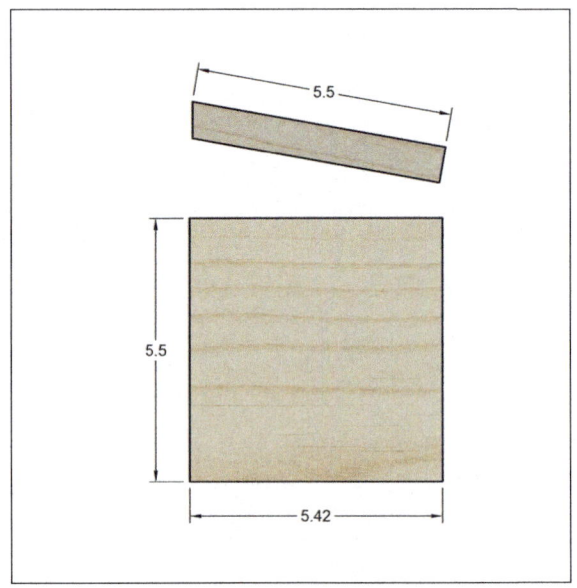

Chapter 7 - Woodworking Plans

Squirrel Feeder

The basic design of the squirrel feeder is similar to the bird house. Again, since the feeder will be outside using rot resistant wood is preferred. In the demonstration photos I'm using a cypress board that was left over from a prior project. The board was a little narrower than I would have liked (it was just over 4" wide), but as I've mentioned a few times you use what you have to make it happen. The plans call for using a board that is 5 1/2" wide.

Just like the bird house there are two pieces that need to be cut that don't have 90-degree cuts, the top of the two sides are cut 10-degrees from

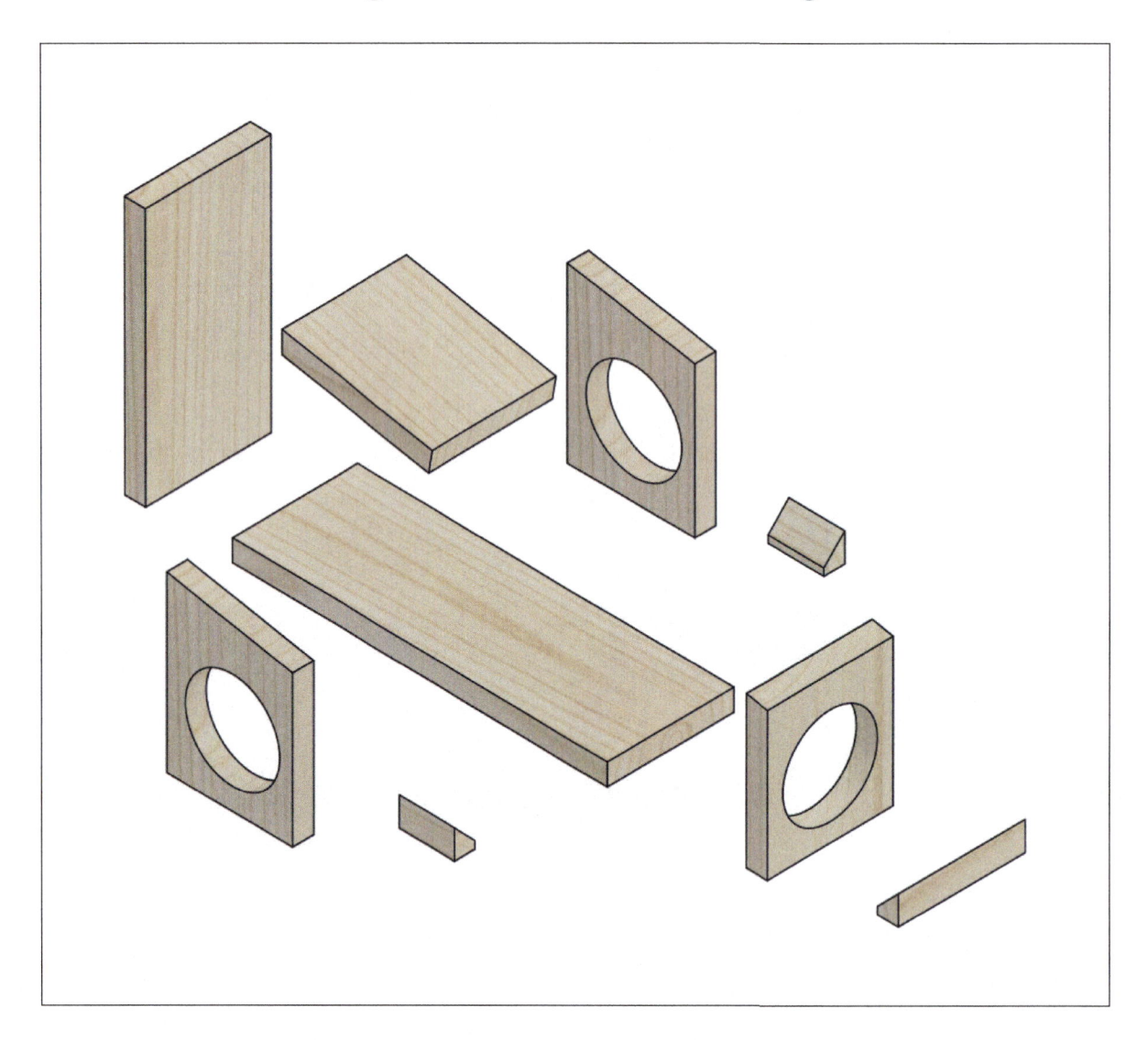

90-degrees. Use a protractor to layout these lines. Also the roof and the front piece have a 10-degree bevel cut.

In the demonstration only glue is used in assembling the squirrel feeder, of course screws or nails could also be used, just remember to predrill if doing so. The first pieces to be assembled are the back and floor. When assembling these pieces, use a square to ensure they are at a perfect 90-degrees.

Next is to attach the sides. The sides need large holes in them to allow the squirrels to enter the feeder. Using a 3" hole saw with the drill is the

Chapter 7 - Woodworking Plans

easiest way to accomplish this. The sides were cut with the 10-degree angle, make sure the higher part of the side is up against the back.

The front needs a hole drilled in it to accommodate the mason jar that will hold the food. I used a 2 1/2" hole saw, but the hole wasn't big enough for the mason jar to fit, so I used a spindle sander to enlarge the hole. If a spindle sander is not available this can be accomplished using a sanding drum for the drill. Of course, the best remedy for this is to use a large enough hole saw in the beginning. The front piece has the 10-degree beveled cut on the top, ensure the high point of the bevel is up against the side pieces. The angle of the side pieces and the bevel of the front piece should be in line with each other.

If hole saws are not available, the holes can be cut out using a jig saw.

Next is to attach the roof. Again, ensure the beveled cut is against the back. The last pieces to be attached are a few pieces that are cut at 45-degrees. These pieces are attached to the bottom piece to ensure the mason jar stays in place. When cutting these pieces it is best to first cut the bevel in a large piece of wood and then cut the pieces to the desired length and width.

Just like the bird house, the back extends past the roof, allowing the feeder to be attached to a pole or tree.

I only fill the mason jar about halfway with bird seed, I figured since squirrels are always stealing the bird seed from the bird feeder they would enjoy it just as much from their own feeder. Just like the bird feeder, the squirrel feeder should not have a finish applied.

To view a video of this project being built go to:

https://youtu.be/6o6Hh6ScswA

Part	Qty.	T	W	L	Mat'l	Notes
Back	1	3/4"	4 1/2"	9"	Pine	
Floor	1	3/4"	4 1/2"	12 3/4"	Pine	
Side	2	3/4"	4 1/2"	4"	Pine	10 degree cut on top for roof slope
Front	1	3/4"	4 1/2"	5 1/4"	Pine	10 degree bevel cut on top edge
Roof	1	3/4"	4 1/2"	5 1/2"	Pine	10 degree bevel cut on back edge
Side Supports	2	3/4"	1"	2"	Pine	45 degree bevel cut on inside
Front Support	1	3/4"	1"	4 1/2"	Pine	45 degree bevel cut on inside

Chapter 7 - Woodworking Plans

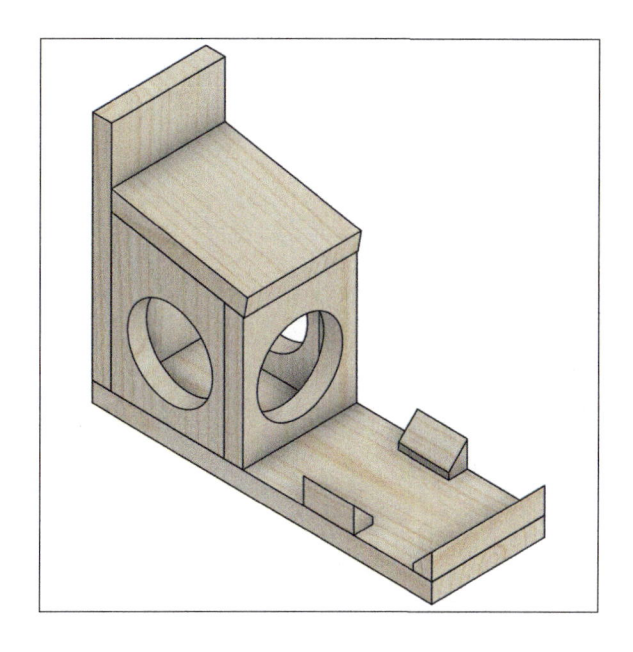

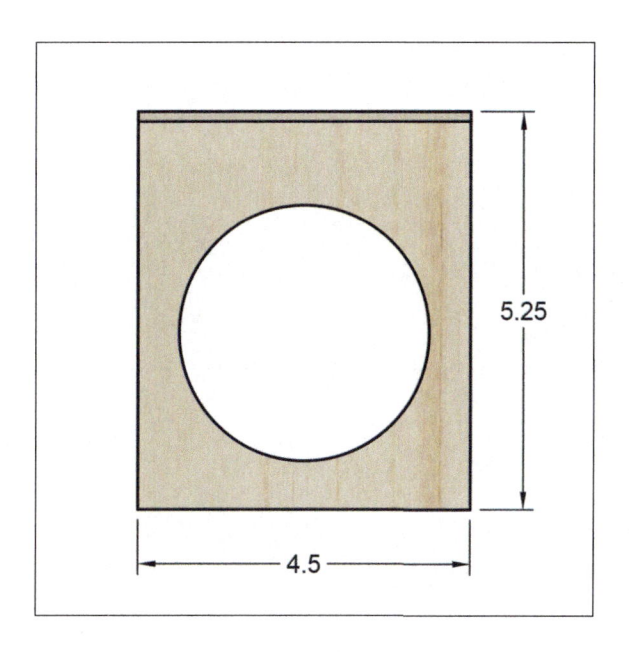

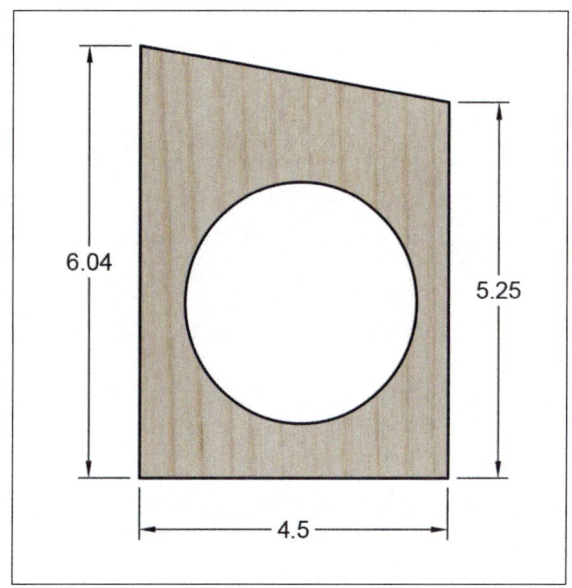

Beginners Guide To Woodworking

4.5

5.42

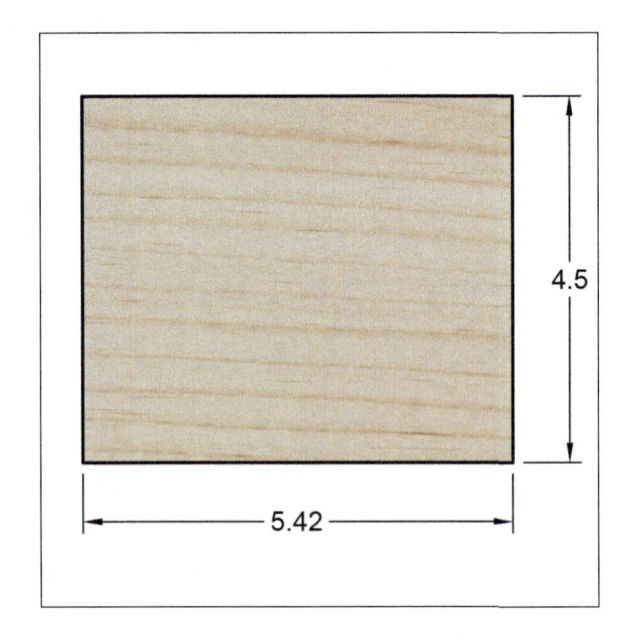

4.5

13.5

Chapter 7 - Woodworking Plans

Paper Towel Holder

This is a very simple paper towel holder that consists of a base and two posts. The purpose of this project is to develop the skill of cutting a round disc. This project can be made using any type of wood, I will be using pine in the demonstration photos. Using a 2' long 8" x 1" board that can be purchased at a big box store will supply the material needed to build the remaining projects.

First, cut a rough piece from the board, the diameter of the base will be 7" (I'm using this measurement because most 8" boards are actually

7 1/2"). When cutting any rough pieces, it's good practice to cut them a little oversized, so I'm cutting my piece at 8".

Next is to layout the circle that will be cutout, a compass is the best tool for this. First is to find the center of the piece, to do this place a straight edge (it can be a ruler or just a straight piece of wood) across opposite corners and draw a line. Do this for both sets of opposing corners, where the lines cross each other is the center of the board. Set the compass to 7" and place the point of the compass in the center of the board and draw the circle.

A jig saw is the best tool to use in cutting out the circle, if cutting it by hand is desired, a coping saw would be a good tool to use. If using a jig saw, make sure the work piece is firmly clamped to the worktable, it is very hard (or impossible) to hold a piece securely with your hands when using a jig saw, not to mention that it is unsafe. Have one third to half the piece hanging over the edge of the table and cut the area that is hanging over, then unclamp the piece, reposition, and reclamp it to continue the cut, do this until the cut is complete. Regardless of which tool is used, ensure the cut is made on the outside of the layout line. 60 or 80 grit sandpaper can be used to

Chapter 7 - Woodworking Plans

remove material that is outside the layout line. If there is a substantial amount of material that needs to be removed a sanding drum attached to a drill is a good option. If using a sanding drum, it is recommended the piece be clamped to the worktable while sanding. The hard edges of the base can also be softened by rounding them over with sandpaper.

Again, I can't say this enough, this is your project, make it any way you want to. If a square base is desired (or any other shape), make it that way. Woodworking plans are just guides.

Now holes need to be drilled to hold the dowels. The tool of choice for this of course is the power drill. There are a couple of options on the type of drill bits that can be used. These are either a spade (also referred to as a paddle) bit or a forstner bit. Spade bits are cheaper but won't provide as clean of a cut as forstner bits. Also, forstner bits are designed more to be used in a drill press but can be used in handheld drills. Drill the holes from the top of the base but don't go all the way through, go down only about half the thickness of the board.

Once the holes are drilled, the dowels can either be glued in place or can be secured using a screw or both. Regardless of the type of drill bit used there will be an indentation in the middle of the hole, using this as a guide to drill the rest of the way through with a 1/8" drill bit. This will be the pilot hole for the screw. Don't forget to counter sink for the screw on the bottom of the base. Do this for both the center and the outside posts.

Insert the dowels in the hole and clamp them so they won't move, and then drill a pilot hole in them going through the hole already drilled on

97

the bottom of the base. Now remove the dowels and apply glue to the dowel and the hole. Insert the dowels and clamp them down, if using a screw, drive it in from the bottom of the base. Clamping the dowels down helps to prevent them from moving. Use the combination square or speed square to make sure the dowels are at a 90 degree angle to the base.

Sand to 220 grit sandpaper prior to applying any finish. As far as finishing the holder, it is up to you whether or not to stain it. Regardless if it is stained or not, a topcoat should be applied, I'm using a wipe-on polyurethane.

The last thing that can be done is to put small rubber pads on the bottom to prevent the holder from sliding around. These are usually self-adhesive, so no glue is required, and they can be found at any big box store.

To view a video of this project being built go to:

https://youtu.be/FzNfv3a3KXU

Part	Qty.	T	W	L	Mat'l	Notes
Base	1	3/4"		7"	Pine	Base is round with 7" diameter
Center Post (Dowl)	1	1"		11 1/4"	Pine	
Outside Post (Dowl)	1	1/2"		6 3/4"	Pine	

Chapter 7 - Woodworking Plans

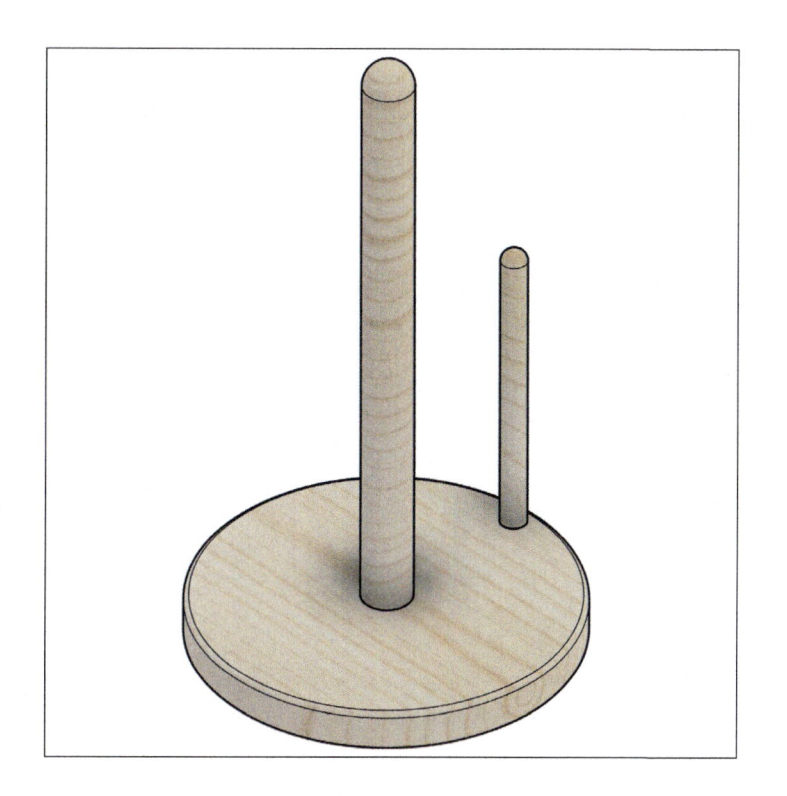

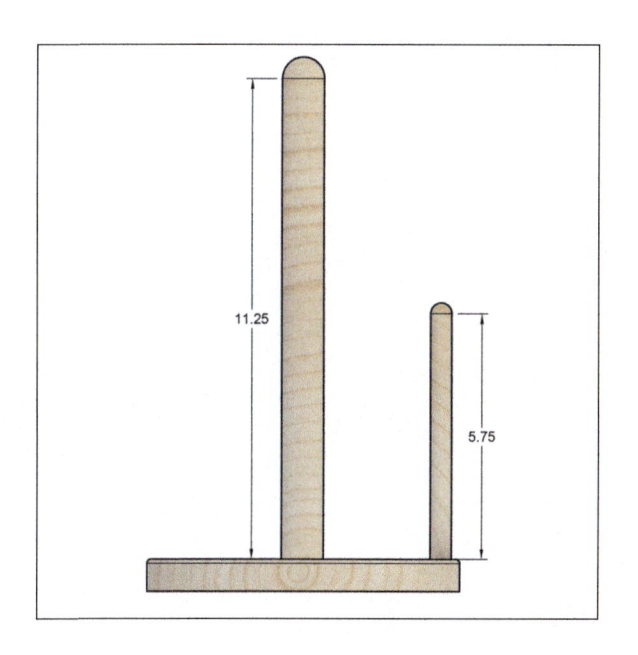

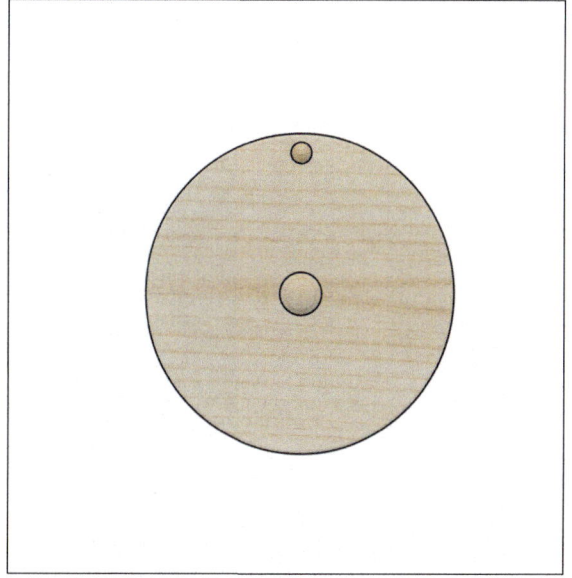

Beginners Guide To Woodworking

Chapter 7 - Woodworking Plans

Napkin Holder

The next project is a napkin holder. This project is designed to develop the woodworker's skill in lining up holes on two different pieces. The base of the napkin holder has two dowels that the top piece slides on. This napkin holder can be made from any kind of wood, again I will be using pine from the same board that was used to build the paper towel holder.

First is to cut the base, the dimensions for the base is 6" x 8". The top is longer than the bottom, but it is also narrower with the dimensions of 3" x 8 1/2".

Beginners Guide To Woodworking

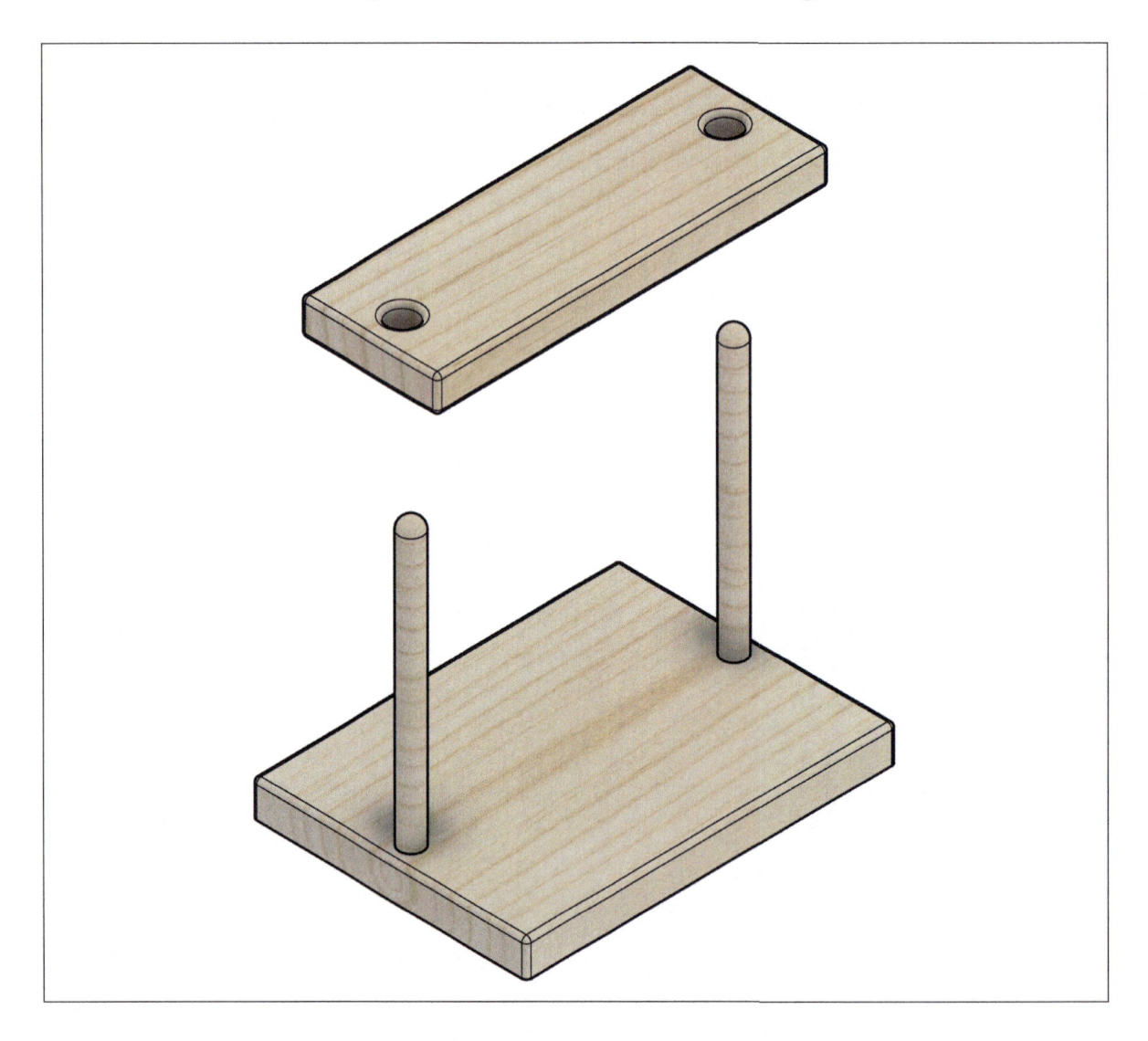

Lining up the holes on a project like this is relatively easy when one of the pieces has the hole go all the way through the piece. First is to drill the holes in the top piece and then use it as a template to mark the location of the holes on the base.

We want the top piece to easily slide down the dowels that will be inserted in the base. To achieve this, drill the holes in the top piece slightly larger than the diameter of the dowels.

With all that being said, lets start drilling. The holes need to be centered down the length of the top piece. Measure half the width of the top, which

Chapter 7 - Woodworking Plans

is 1 1/2", and use the combination square to mark it down the length. Next, determine how far in from the ends the holes need to be. Using a napkin as a reference (the average paper napkin is 6.5"). Subtract this from the length of the top and divide the result in half. This gives a measurement of 1", this is the maximum distance the holes should be from the edge of the top. Decrease the distance to allow for irregularities in the napkins, 1/8" on each side (for a combined total of 1/4") should be enough. This gives the location of where the outside of the holes need to be, but the center of the holes is what is needed. The holes will be drilled using a 5/16" drill bit, divide that in half and subtract it from the measurement. This gives us a measurement just under 3/4", rounding it up to 3/4", this will be the mark on the top to drill for the holes. There are probably easier ways to determine this, but this works for me (and I'm not a mathematician).

Once both holes are drilled in the top piece, it can be used as a template to drill the holes in the base. Draw a line down the middle of the base from side to side. The pieces can now be lined up by looking through the holes that were drilled in the top. Since the top is longer than the base ensure there is an equal amount hanging over each side. Once the pieces are lined up clamp them together so they won't move. Since the holes needed in the base are smaller than the holes in the top the same drill bit cannot not be used to drill the holes, but this drill bit can be used to mark the location of the hole, place the drill bit in the hole and press down on it just enough for it to make a mark on the base. Once this is done the pieces can be unclamped and the holes can be drilled at the marks using the smaller drill bit (one that is the same size of the dowel). Remember to only drill about half way through.

Just like the paper towel holder the dowels can be assembled either by just gluing them in or by securing them with screws or both. If using screws, use the indention left in the center of the hole by the bit to predrill for the screw. Place the dowel in the hole and predrill the dowel through the hole in the bottom of the base. Don't forget to counter sink for the screw. Remove the dowel, add glue to the hole and dowel and replace it in the hole. Clamp the dowel and drive in the screw. Use either the combination square or speed square to ensure the dowels are at 90 degrees to the base. If assembling with only glue, keep it clamped until the glue dries.

Round over the sharp edges with 60 or 80 grit sandpaper. Then sand the entire holder to 220 prior to applying any finish. It is up to you as to whether or not to stain the holder, I will only be applying a top coat of wipe-on polyurethane. The final thing is to put small rubber pads on the bottom to prevent the holder from sliding around. These are usually self-adhesive, so no glue is required, and they can be found at any big box store.

To view a video of this project being built go to:

https://youtu.be/FzNfv3a3KXU

Chapter 7 - Woodworking Plans

Part	Qty.	T	W	L	Mat'l	Notes
Base	1	3/4"	6"	8"	Pine	
Top	1	3/4"	3"	8 1/2"	Pine	
Post (Dowl)	2	1/4"		6"	Pine	

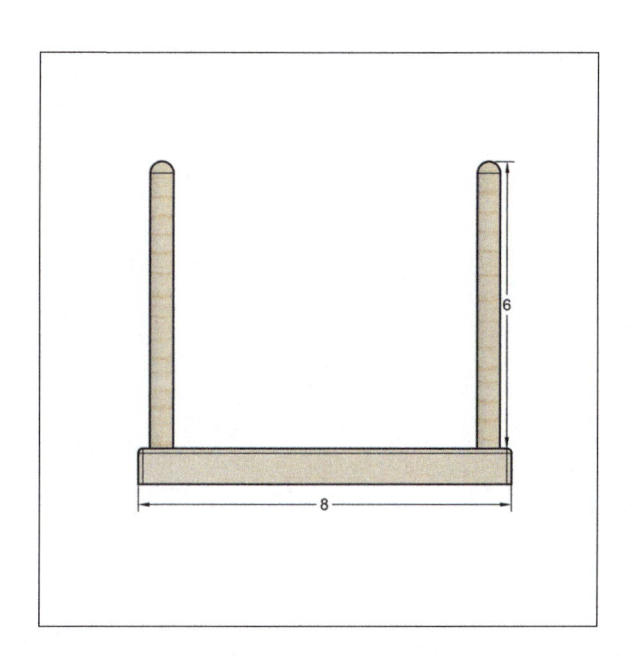

105

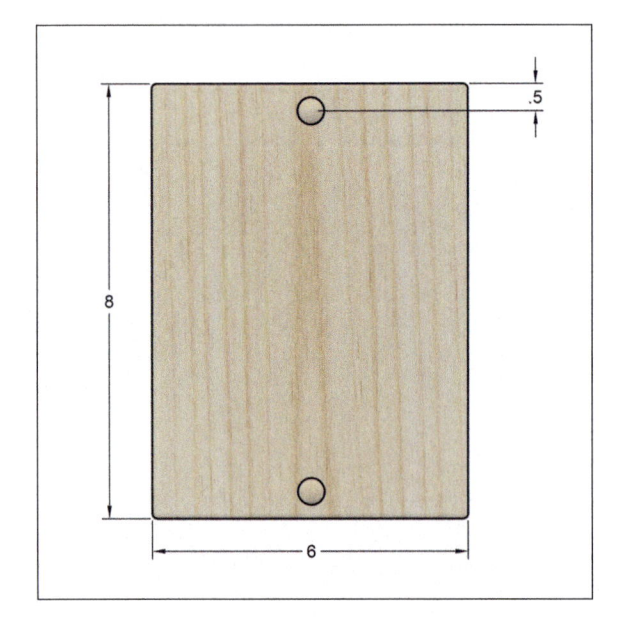

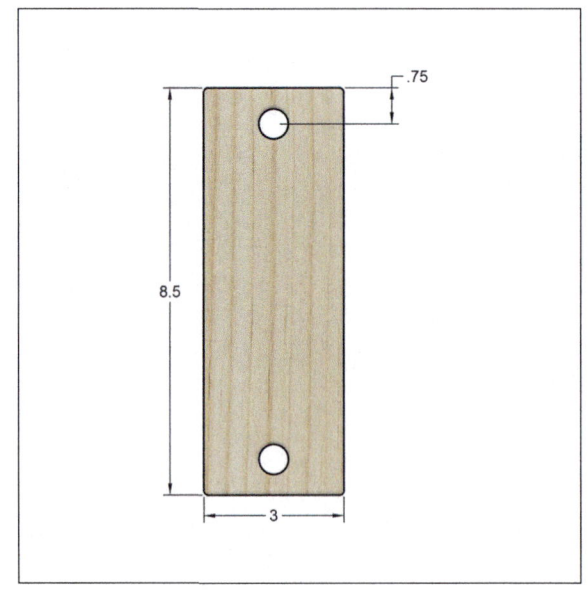

Beginners Guide To Woodworking

Chapter 7 - Woodworking Plans

Taco Shell Holder

The taco shell holder is a very simple project. It consists of a base with partitions to hold the taco shells up right so you can make your tacos without making a mess. This project is designed to be assembled by using spacer blocks which eliminates the need to measure each time a piece is attached.

There should be enough wood remaining from the 8" x 1" board used to make the paper towel and napkin holders to complete this project. Cut a piece that is 14 1/2" long by 4" wide, this will be the base of the holder. Since the holder is relatively narrow this is another example of making sure the grain runs in the correct direction, the grain should run along the length of the board. The partitions will be cut at a height of 2 1/2" by 4" long. The direction of the grain is not crucial with the partitions, as the grain can run in either direction, but it should run in the same direction on all the pieces (this is more for esthetics purposes than anything else).

The plan calls for using six partition pieces, creating a holder that will hold five taco shells. This can be adjusted to your own preference by adding or reducing the number of partitions. An average taco shell is 2" wide, so the distance between each partition should be that distance, a spacer block will be cut to this dimension.

The dimensions of the taco shell holder were determined in order to allow a taco shell to fit snugly without moving and then to be easily removed by allowing the taco shell to hang out of the holder a little. The dimensions can easily be adjusted to accommodate larger or smaller taco shells. As I consistently say, woodworking plans are just a guide.

In cutting the partitions start by cutting a strip of wood the width of the base. Then cut the partition pieces to size. In the demonstration photos I rounded the corners, this is not necessary, but it enhances the overall look of the holder. A trick that makes rounding the corners quick an easy is to use painter's tape and CA (super) glue to temporarily glue the pieces together so all the corners can be rounded at the same time. A belt sander is the perfect tool to do

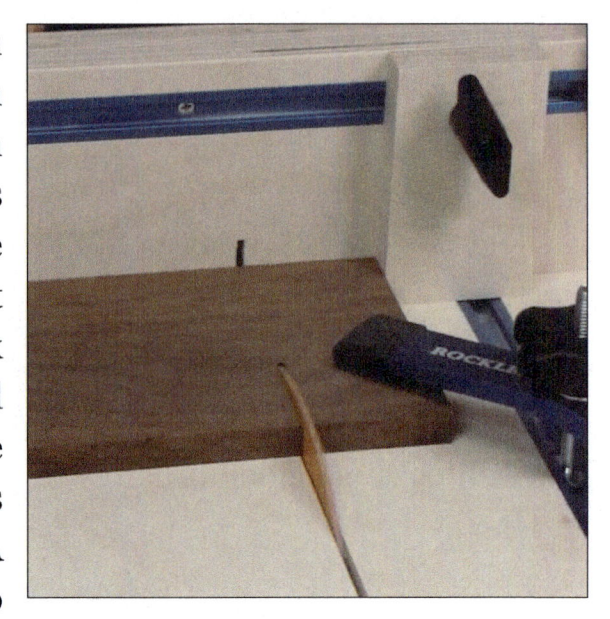

Chapter 7 - Woodworking Plans

this but can also be accomplished by using a drum sander for the drill.

Once all the pieces are cut it is ready for assembly. Assembly will be done using only glue, since the hold will be used in the kitchen and will probably need a washing periodically a water proof glue should be used. The end partitions are the first to be assembled, ensure they are flush with the end of the base and clamp them down. Use a 2" spacer bock to place the next partition, the end pieces should remain clamped while doing this or they have the possibility to move (remember it can take up to 24 hours for the glue to fully cure). Once the second partition piece is clamped remove the spacer block and repeat for the next partition piece. If there are not enough clamps available to have all the partitions clamped at once, ensure the pieces have been clamped to at least allow the glue to dry before unclamping them.

There may be some glue squeeze out that needs to be removed. Before applying a finish, sand it to at least 180 grit sandpaper. A food safe finish should be applied, this can be mineral oil, butcherblock oil, bees wax, etc.

To view a video of this project being built go to:

https://youtu.be/HPb-VdjmdCw

Beginners Guide To Woodworking

Part	Qty.	T	W	L	Mat'l	Notes
Base	1	3/4"	4"	14 1/2"	Pine	
Partitions	6	3/4"	2 1/4"	4"	Pine	Round over top corners

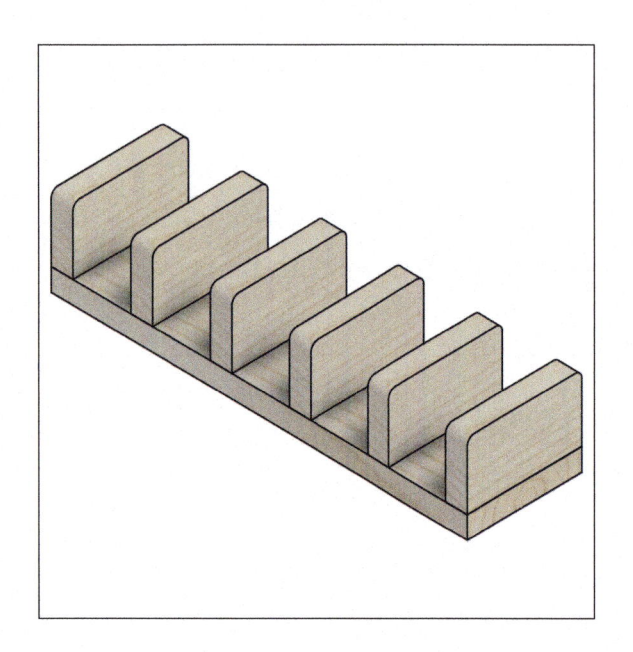

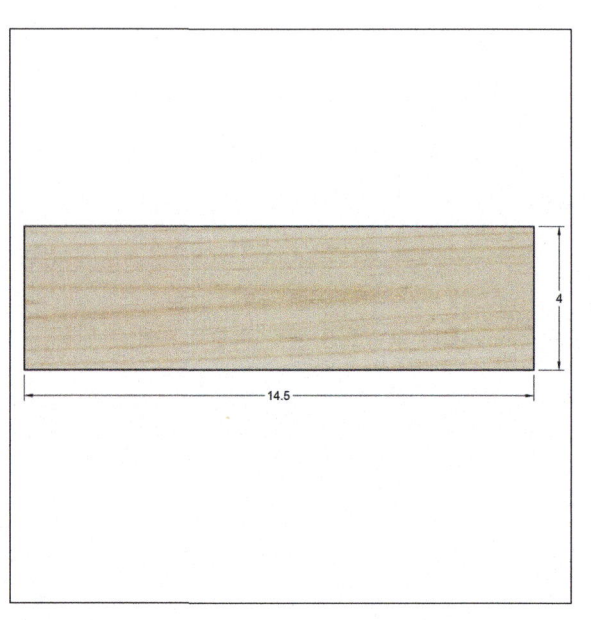

Chapter 7 - Woodworking Plans

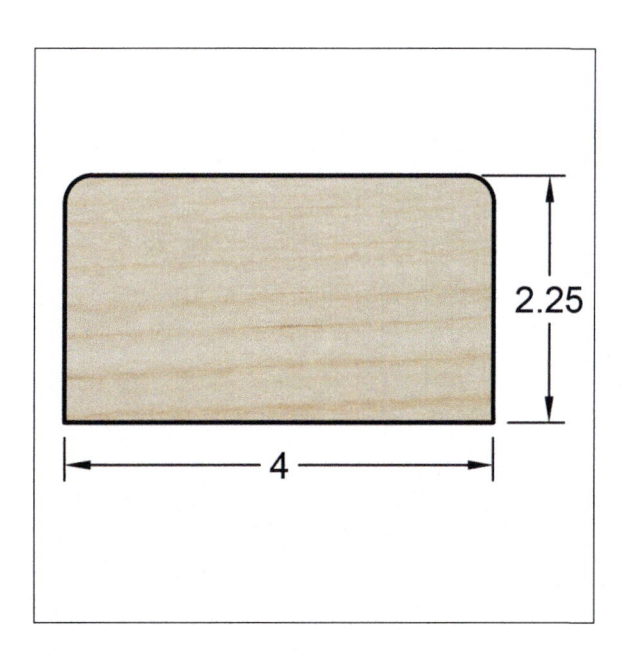

Beginners Guide To Woodworking

References

Anglia Tool Centre (2017); The History Of Power Tools; www.angliatoolcentre.co.uk/blog/history-power-tools.html.

Baylor, Chris (2019); Woodworking Safety Rules Every Woodworker Should Know; The Spruce Crafts; www.thesprucecrafts.com/safety-rules-every-woodworker-should-know-3536833.

Baylor, Chris (2019); 13 Types of Wood Joinery; The Spruce Crafts; www.thesprucecrafts.com/wood-joinery-types-3536631.

Canadian Centre for Occupational Health and Safety (n.d.); Woodworking Machines – General Safety Tips; www.ccohs.ca/oshanswers/safety_haz/woodwork/gen_safe.html.

Chaudhry, Raj (2019); Everything You Ever Wanted To Know About Wood Glue; Cottage Life; cottagelife.com/design-diy/everything-you-ever-wanted-to-know-about-wood-glue.

Farnsworth, Joshua (2022); How To Choose Hand Saws For Wood Working; Wood and Shop; woodandshop.com/woodworking-hand-tool-buying-guide-handsaws.

Fine Woodworking (n.d); www.finewoodworking.com.

Forest Service (1972); Wood Handbook: Wood as an Engineering Material; United States Department of Agriculture.

Johnson Level (n.d.); Combination Squares; www.johnsonlevel.com/News/CombinationSquares.

Minwax (n.d.); Staining Interior Wood; www.minwax.com/how-to-finish-wood/staining-wood.

Niggl, John (2018); Wood Warping And How To Prevent It; Intouch; www.intouch-quality.com/blog/wood-warping-and-how-to-prevent-it.

Popular Woodworking (n.d.); www.popularwoodworking.com.

Schwarz, Christopher (2003, Aug); Lusting For Lumber; Popular Woodworking.

Taylor, Glenda and Vila, Bob (2020); 7 Types Of Saws Every DIYer Should Get to Know; Bob Vila; www.bobvila.com/articles/types-of-saws.

The Handyman's Daughter (n.d); www.thehandymansdaughter.com/beginning-woodworking.

Wonkee Donkee Tools (n.d.); Crosscut Saw Teeth vs Rip Saw Teeth; www.wonkeedonkeetools.co.uk/handsaws/what-is-the-difference-between-crosscut-and-rip-teeth.

Woodcraft Magazine (n.d.); www.woodcraft.com/pages/magazine.

Wood Magazine (n.d); www.woodmagazine.com.

Woodsmith (n.d.); www.woodsmith.com.

Woodworkers Guild of America (n.d.); www.wwgoa.com.

Woodworkers Journal (n.d.); www.woodworkersjournal.com.

Printed in Great Britain
by Amazon